John A. O'Connor
Digital Art 2013-2020

White Lies Matters

iUniverse books may be ordered through booksellers or by contacting:

iUniverse
1663 Liberty Drive
Bloomington, IN 47403
www.iuniverse.com
844-349-9409

Because of the dynamic nature of the Internet, any web addresses or links contained in this book may have changed since publication and may no longer be valid. The views expressed in this work are solely those of the author and do not necessarily reflect the views of the publisher, and the publisher hereby disclaims any responsibility for them.

Any people depicted in stock imagery provided by Getty Images are models,
and such images are being used for illustrative purposes only.
Certain stock imagery © Getty Images.

ISBN: 978-1-6632-1095-1 (sc)
ISBN: 978-1-6632-1096-8 (e)

Library of Congress Control Number: 2020919964

Print information available on the last page.

iUniverse rev. date: 12/08/2020

Foreward

John O'Connor's "White Lies Matter: Decoding American Deceptionalism"

By Michael Wilson

Artist/art professor John A. O'Connor characterizes his series White Lies Matter: Decoding American Deceptionalism as "a history of American hypocrisy." Using the image of the slate as a consistent base, White Lies Matter ranges across historical and contemporary America, touching down at flashpoints of inequality, misunderstanding, and conflict. From the gradual decay of national institutions to more immediate political crises, O'Connor's project traverses a list of illegalities and cover-ups, oppressions and suppressions, tracing links between individuals and institutions in positions of influence. It begins with Christopher Columbus and the First Thanksgiving—mythologies that crumble very easily by now—and moves on through the contradictory and belated embedding of religion in the nation's founding documents, to the calamitous installation of Donald Trump as its 45th president.

White Lies Matter: Decoding American Deceptionalism reveals the deceptions, lies, and cynicism of America and the "fake news" and "alt- facts" that permeate contemporary society.

Note: Michael Wilson is a New York-based writer and editor and the author of How to Read Contemporary Art: Experiencing the Art of the 21st Century (New York: Abrams, 2013).

Acknowledgements

Artists Hieronymus Bosch, Francisco Goya, and William Hogarth, whose political discourse as embodied in their work, inspired me to develop this series that reveals the true United States of America. During that process, I took a more thorough look at American history and acknowledge all of the sources that I have cited whose scholarly work helped me create images that uncover myths and reveal rarely discussed layers of American history.

To my wife Mallory, whose encouragement throughout our time together (now more than fifty-seven wonderful years) I express my lifelong gratitude for her support and encouragement. Specifically, with regard to White Lies Matter, I owe her many thanks for the numerous hours of discussion and suggestions as I developed the concept for this undertaking starting in earnest in 2013, and for her enthusiasm and critical comments about the development of the sixty images that comprise this series. She also was the first editor for the text that follows each work of art, and oversaw the process of securing Michael Wilson's essay on White Lies Matter. She handled the details of bringing this book to fruition with iUniverse who published this manuscript both in print and as a fixed format e-book.

I also am grateful for my son Christopher's valuable comments on both the text and images in this work.

Thanks are also in order for Katharine T. Carter of Katharine T. Carter and Associates and Jen Dragon for working with me to create an online version of White Lies Matter, and Anne Taylor, my final editor, whose very helpful feedback and corrections helped me significantly.

And finally, I would like to thank one of my former students, Patrick Grigsby, who once said that when I was talking about my digital art, people would suddenly be learning how to look at my art because the oral descriptions provided the necessary trigger to get people to really think about the art. That is what it is all about!

John A. O'Connor, Gainesville, Florida, August 31, 2020

Plate 1

John A. O'Connor, *White Lies Matter: Decoding American Deceptionalism*
2017-18. Digital Image, 21 x 17 in.

> If you tell a lie big enough and keep repeating it, people will eventually come to believe it. The lie can be maintained only for such time as the State can shield the people from the political, economic and/or military consequences of the lie. It thus becomes vitally important for the State to use all of its powers to repress dissent, for the truth is the mortal enemy of the lie, and thus by extension, the truth is the greatest enemy of the State.
>
> —Joseph Goebbels

White Lies Matter: Decoding American Deceptionalism is a visual history of American hypocrisy.

"The Illusory Truth Effect: Exploring Implicit and Explicit Memory Influences on Consumer Judgments" states, "Repetition does not seem like a sound basis for determining truth, but researchers have consistently found that people rate repeated statements as more true than non-repeated statements. This effect is known as the illusory truth effect and appears to be quite persistent."[1]

The Illusory truth effect affirms that what Joesph Goebbels, the Nazi Minister of Propaganda from 1933-45—and one of Adolf Hitler's closest associates—said is quite true! If a lie is repeated over and over, the chance that it will be accepted as truth increases each time the lie is repeated.

This phenomenon didn't just occur. It wasn't the result of Stephen Colbert's constant battering us with "truthiness." The idea of repeating a lie to convince someone that it was the truth goes back to Roman times and was also used by Napoleon, Ronald Reagan, and probably every politician and advertiser who was aware of its effects.[2]

This introduction is based on my research on the illusory truth effect, lies, and the "illusion of reality"—and it also provides the context for the "decoding" that occurs on the following pages.

Beginning in the early 1960s, John A. O'Connor, "the punning, painting, pedagogue" began a series of paintings, drawings, and works on paper that included satire, social criticism, and anti-mainstream commentary on a variety of issues. Taking his lead from artists like Hieronymus Bosch *(The Garden of Earthly Delights, The Last Judgment);* William Hogarth *(A Harlot's Progress, A Rake's Progress);* and Francisco José de Goya y Lucientes *(Los Disparates [The follies, The Proverbs, and/or The Dreams]; Los Disastres de la Guerra;* and, especially *Los Caprichos),* O'Connor initiated a second side to his better-known Bay Area Figurative work. Including word-plays made with stencils, irreverent dialog, and a take on the more serious works by Jasper Johns, O'Connor started to develop a group of themes and images that would recur throughout his career and subsequently lead to the current digital art series, *White Lies Matter: Decoding American Deceptionalism.*

This series of "fake slates" explores many popular misconceptions that we all share about what is really going on in our lives. From early American treatment of the native population to a symbol of the only Irish pub on communist soil at Guantánamo Bay, Cuba "where it don't gitmo better than this." After careful consideration, Bill Clinton's "little blue dress" episode looks down-right insignificant when compared to JFK's real exploits. What is the real story behind Obama's "red line in Syria?" Other issues include the ubiquitous "1%." Is its rule "The New Normal?" What about the CEO of BP whose infamous remark following the disastrous Gulf Oil Spill was, "I want my life back"—as if his life were the one at risk, and the only one that really mattered. There is also the re-revelation of NASA'S Nazis. Who alive today remembers them, or how our government officials hid their illegal actions from then-President Truman while importing some of the greatest war criminals the world had ever witnessed?

Numerous other issues are also revealed, or uncovered—such as the government's role in suppressing contraception by using the U.S. Postal Service as its agent. The support of blood libel, the yellow cake incident, the cover-ups at Abu Ghraib, and many more ask **you** tough questions about what you really know about "the greatest country on earth."

White Lies Matter: Decoding American Deceptionalism reveals the deceptions, lies, and cynicism of America and the "fake news" and "alt-facts" that permeate contemporary society.

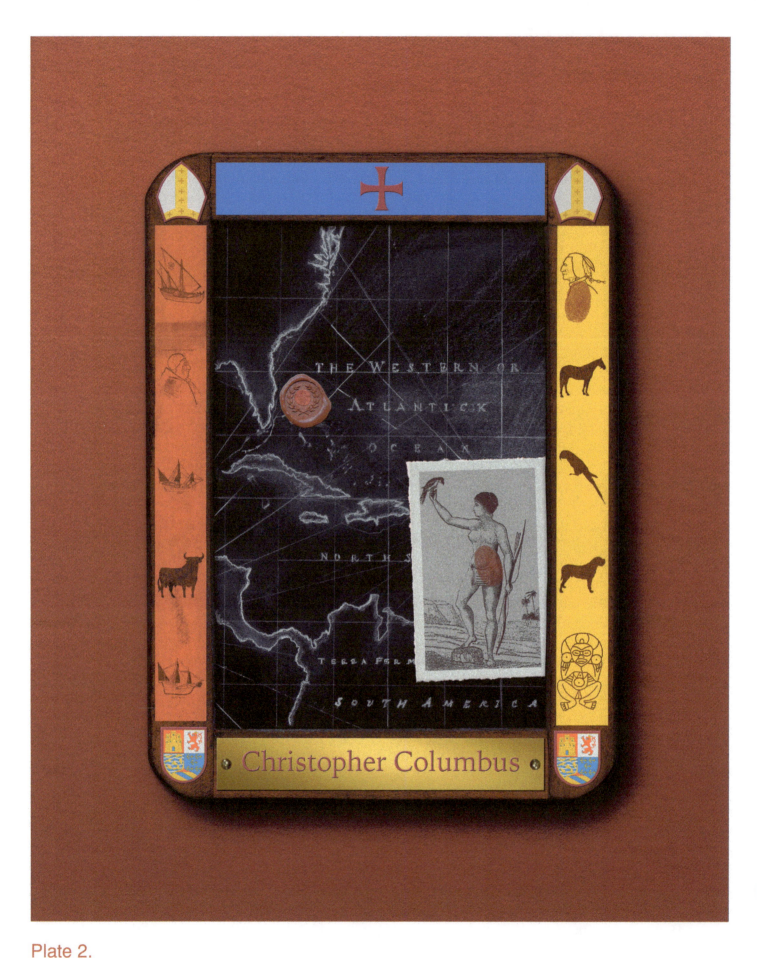

Plate 2.
John A. O'Connor, *Columbus Discovered America, Right?* 2018. Digital Image, 21 x 17 in.

WHITE LIES MATTER

For decades, American schoolchildren parroted the rhyme "In fourteen hundred ninety-two Columbus sailed the ocean blue."[1] While it appears that there is virtually no agreement on who really wrote this poem (it's much longer than the opening line), it seems to have literally infected American history.

So, did Columbus really discover America? Well, no! He apparently never even set foot on any part of the Americas—unless you want to argue that the islands in the Caribbean—the West Indies—are a part of America. Ironically, they are called the West Indies because Columbus thought he had discovered the East Indies—and called its residents "Indians."[2]

Columbus made four voyages to the "new world," but it was finding gold that drove him and the early Spanish colonists. (He did not attempt to prove that the world was round by his voyages as is commonly believed. Most of the people of his time had given up on that idea much earlier.) In order to mine this precious mineral, they utilized the native population as slaves. Subsequently, the original inhabitants of the West Indies were virtually exterminated by European colonists who infected them with various diseases to which they had no immunity or by extreme exploitation and overworking them.[3]

Columbus' story becomes even more incredible when the Pope "gave" the Americas to Spain! Following Columbus' discovery, Pope Alexander VI issued a May 4, 1493, papal bull granting official ownership of the New World to Ferdinand and Isabella. To these monarchs, the Pope declared:

> We of our own motion, and not at your solicitation, do give, concede, and assign for ever to you and your successors, all the islands, and main lands, discovered; and which may hereafter, be discovered, towards the west and south; whether they be situated towards India, or towards any other part whatsoever, and give you absolute power in them.[4]

To make Columbus' discovery of America even more unlikely, one needs only to refer to Leif Eriksson who is generally regarded as the first European to set foot on North America sometime around the year 1000—almost 500 years before Columbus discovered America.[5]

But was Eriksson really the first European to make landfall in the Americas or was it the Solutreans? And, if so, when? If this story were true, it would appear that they arrived from Europe more than 20,000 years ago. And that would be a godsend for white supremacists and the "Make America Great Again" crowd—for it would imply that Europeans and not Indians first settled this country.[6]

And, although many Americans continue to celebrate Columbus on his own very special occasion—Columbus Day—originally proclaimed a national holiday by U.S. President Franklin Delano Roosevelt in 1937[7]—other, more informed Americans celebrate Indigenous Peoples Day. In spite of what passes for "authentic American history," Columbus' real legacy was "colonialism, slavery, and the destruction of peoples and cultures."[8]

Plate 3

John A. O'Connor, *The First Thanksgiving,* 2018. Digital Image, 21 x 17 in. 2017)

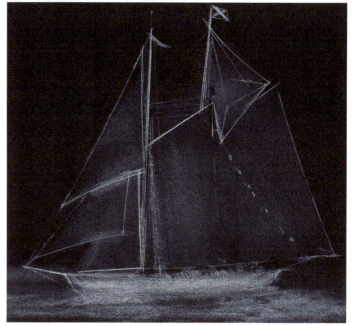

As children, most of us learned that Pilgrims on the Mayflower arrived at Plymouth Rock in 1620. Many Americans today believe that they were the first settlers in what is now the United States. Unprepared for the harsh winter, they, supposedly, were saved by the friendly natives, who gave them food and taught them how to plant corn.[1]

The following autumn, during their first harvest in the New World, they had a feast to commemorate the hardships they had survived, and Pilgrim and Indian joined hands in a glorious celebration.

Of course, the reality was quite different, since the Spanish had arrived much earlier. No, Christopher Columbus, an Italian explorer in service to Spain after being refused by England and Portugal, didn't "discover" America in 1492. Seeking a trade route to Asia, Columbus landed in what is now the Bahamas.[2]

The real story is far more cruel, murderous, and genocidal. Years before the Pilgrims arrived, Spanish settlers and their African slaves established a very small town in what is now South Carolina. But instead of the glorious celebrations and wonderful Thanksgivings, there were apparently many misgivings, including disease, fights with the Indians, and a slave revolt, followed by the Spanish evacuation back to Haiti. Consequently, the first non-native settlers in the U.S. were black Africans! (Make America Great Again?)[3]

Elsewhere, British fishermen had introduced a plague that swept through the tribes of coastal New England and wiped out nearly ninety-six percent of the entire population before the Pilgrims even landed. There were reportedly so many bodies that settlers would leave the towns rather than deal with them—only to introduce the bug to the next tribe they encountered. In James Loewen's article on Thanksgiving, he quotes Howard Simpson, "Villages lay in ruins because there was no one to tend them. The ground was strewn with the skulls and the bones of thousands of Indians who had died and none was left to bury them."[4]

There's also evidence that the Pilgrims already knew about the plague, and so chose Cape Cod because they knew that the Indians had already been wiped out, leaving cleared lands and cornfields ripe for the taking. Even worse, the Pilgrims would steal food and tools from any Indians left alive, who were too weak to fight back. But the settlers in Virginia were actually eating the Indians,[5] so I guess the Pilgrims weren't that bad by comparison. Yes, I did say eating them.[6]

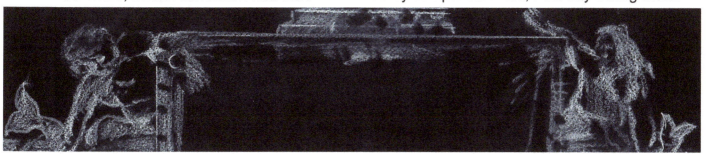

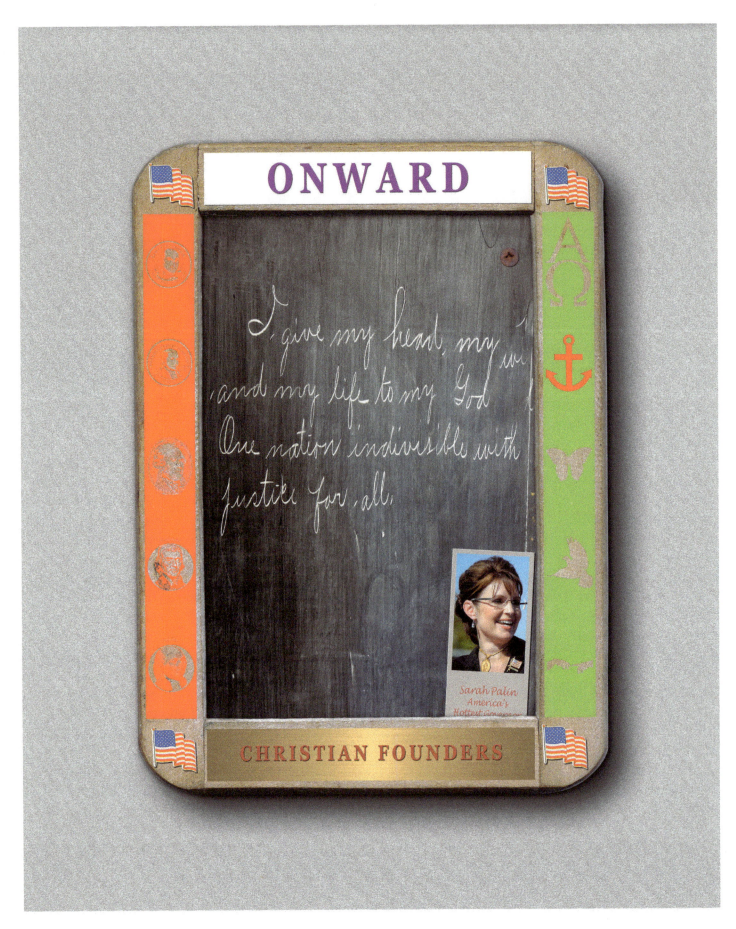

Plate 4
John A. O'Connor, *Onward Christian Founders,* 2018. Digital Image, 21 x 17 in.

There is not even one reference in the Constitution of the United States to " 'God' or 'the Almighty' or any euphemism for a higher power."[1] The U.S. Declaration of Independence (1776) states that the government derives it power from "the consent of the governed." There are, however, four references to "higher powers" in the document, but the author infers that they never implied "a role for a god in government."[2]

In the Articles of Confederation, the term "Great Governor of the World" occurs once, but "just as the Articles of Confederation give no authority to religion in civil matters, so too does the document deny any authority of government in matters of faith."[3]

In Article VI of The Constitution of the United States (1787), the one reference to religion is "[N]o religious Test shall ever be required as a Qualification to any Office or public Trust under the United States."[4]

The Federalist Papers (1787-88) were written by John Jay, Alexander Hamilton, and James Madison, and religion is only mentioned in terms of keeping it out of government and government out of religion. The author then concludes, "We are not a Christian nation."[5]

Jumping ahead to modern times, Sarah Palin reminds us that the phrase, "under God" in the Pledge of Allegiance "was good enough for the founding fathers, its [sic] good enough for me. . . ."[6] Since that phrase was put into the Pledge in 1954, that means Hamilton would have been 197 years old, Madison 203, and Jay 209.

But what about, "In God We trust"? Try 1861, the Civil War, and the U.S. government's pandering to the National Reform Association. (NRA!)

Ironically, while most Americans, and most of America's "Real and Fake Media" denounce Islamic Sharia Law, a significant number of both apparently want and would support Christian Law. In 1954, one Ralph Flanders (no, not the one in *The Simpsons*)—a Senator from independent Bernie Sander's Vermont—proposed The Flanders Amendment to the U.S. Constitution. It stated that, "This nation devoutly recognizes the authority and law of Jesus Christ, Savior and Ruler of nations, through whom are bestowed the blessings of almighty God." [7]

Sarah Palin
America's

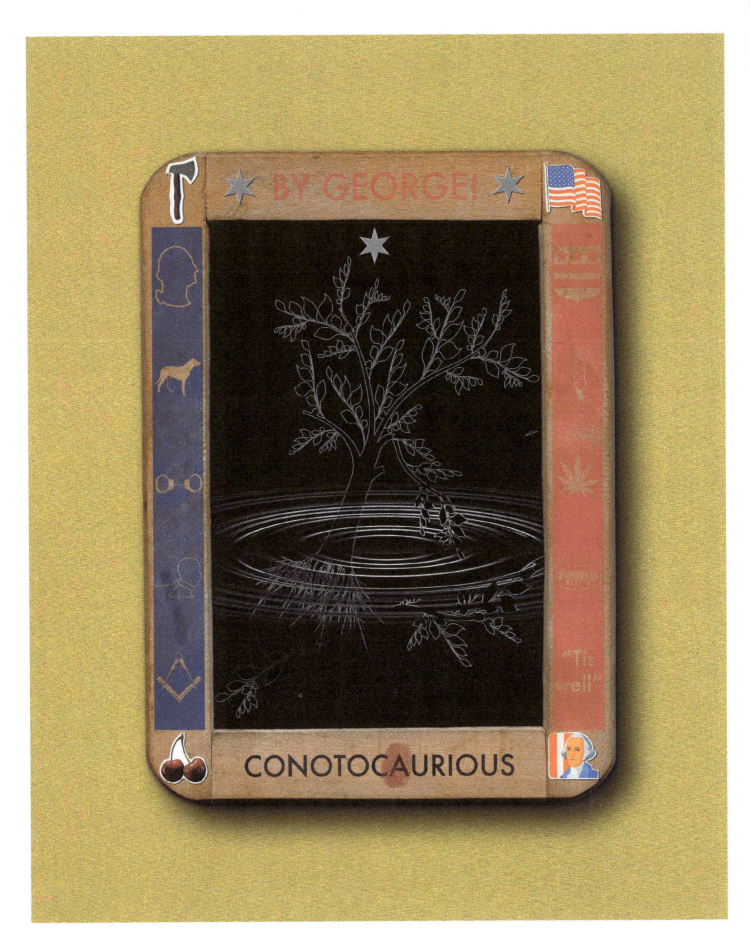

Plate 5
John A. O'Connor, *By George,* 2017. Digital Image, 21 x 17 in.

WHITE LIES MATTER

The cherry tree myth is, undoubtedly, the most well-known and longest enduring legend about George Washington.

In the original version of this long-celebrated myth, when young George was six years old he received a hatchet as a gift. What to do?

Well, George apparently—and with great gusto—whacked up his father's beloved cherry tree. When his father, Augustine, discovered what George had done, he became quite angry and confronted him. Young George—supposedly—bravely said, "I cannot tell a lie. . .I did cut it with my hatchet."[1]

Apparently overwhelmed, "Washington's father embraced him and rejoiced that his son's honesty was worth more than a thousand trees."[2]

Who invented this myth and why did it endure? Well, it was concocted by one Mason Locke Weems who has been described "as an itinerant minister and bookseller."[3] Generally known as Parson Weems, he first published *The Life of Washington* in 1800, but he didn't include the cherry tree legend until the fifth edition in 1806. Weems evidently was a wise and shrewd salesman because he had a plan to use this elevation of honesty as a great private virtue to sell the American public on a hero the people were anxious to read about. In this way, Weems was able to emphasize virtues that showed Washington "as the perfect role model, especially for young Americans."[4] By showing that Washington's great public achievements were the result of his private integrity, Weems was able to portray the private side of a public hero—the inside story of a man about whom the masses knew little.

Ironically, it was another minister and college professor, one William Holmes McGuffey, who in his famous *McGuffey's Readers,* developed a series of grammar school textbooks that retold the cherry tree myth as a children's story for over twenty years in his *Eclectic Second Reader*. More than 120 million copies of these "readers" were sold during the century that they remained in print.[5]

Then, in the 1830s the cherry tree myth was further ingrained in the American fabric by no less than P. T. Barnum. He purchased an elderly slave woman whom he advertised was the 161 year old woman who raised George Washington. Apparently her success at telling believable stories was based on her age.[6]

By George, no wonder the cherry tree myth has endured!

Do you know who was Conotocaurious? Conotocaurious is "an Algonquian name that translated to 'town taker' or "devourer of villages." It was the name George Washington used when he referred to himself in negotiations with the "Nations of Indians."[7] That name, ironically, is not exactly the name one would expect to be used when referring to the "father of America."

Plate 6
John A. O'Connor, *Measuring Value,* 2016-17. Digital Image, 21 x 17 in.

WHITE LIES MATTER

The Declaration of Independence states, "We hold these truths to be self-evident, that all men are created equal. . . ." American Exceptionalism indeed!

America's most fought for and admired values:

- Freedom
- Equality
- Democracy
- Champion of the little guy
- Helper of the oppressed
- Defender against tyranny
- Capitalism
- Independence
- Strength
- Rightness and righteousness
- Manifest destiny
- God
- Freedom of religion

"Capitalism and strength have made America great, but they have generated their own set of inequalities. Our wealth is unequaled, but Jesus taught that our faith should make wealth meaningless. Equality is a wonderful ideal, but frankly, not everyone is created equal. Freedom is fine until we see our vast money-obsessed entertainment and happiness apparatus assaulting us with base immorality, cowardly news, and stupidity."[1]

The images in the left and right panels represent various countries' symbol/sign for money based on a list of the highest value world currencies.

Plate 7

John A. O'Connor, *The Golden Rule,* 2016-17. Digital Image, 21 x 17 in.

WHITE LIES MATTER

The desire of gold is not for gold. It is for
the means of freedom and benefit.
——Ralph Waldo Emerson

"He who has the gold makes the rules," is widely attributed to Brant Parker and Johnny Hart for the comment in the fourth panel of their May 3, 1965 comic strip, *Wizard of Id.*[1] However, there are many other claimants to this quote, and it has had many other manifestations.

Of course, the original meaning of The Golden Rule, "Do unto others as you would have them do unto you," is quite different. Appearing in antiquity, it eventually occurs, in varying forms, in nearly all religions. Ironically, a number of philosophers have criticized the rule on numerous levels—one in particular that has great relevance today. For example, if a terrorist with no aversion to his or her own death wanted to die because death would lead to martyrdom, then this "rule" *could* appear to justify the killing of others. Why? Because the Golden Rule is not singular. It has at least two forms: positive and negative.[2]

There are also numerous criticisms of the criticisms of The Golden Rule. Irony exists here also because one could easily contend that, throughout human history, most people have never tried to apply the rule, let alone live by it.

The images depicted on the panels on this slate have a very specific relationship to gold and its influence both as a symbol and metaphor. For example, why do we seek wealth? Why is or was there a gold standard? Why did the U.S. go off the gold standard? Does money buy happiness? The great philosopher, Arthur Schopenhauer once said, "Money is like sea-water: The more we drink the thirstier we become; and the same is true of fame."[3]

Friedrich Nietzsche once asked, "But tell me: how did gold get to be the highest value? Because it is uncommon and useless and gleaming and gentle in its brilliance; it always gives itself. Only as an image of the highest virtue did gold get to be the highest value. The giver's glance gleams like gold. A golden brilliance concludes peace between the moon and the sun. Uncommon is the highest virtue and useless, it is gleaming and gentle in its brilliance: a gift-giving virtue is the highest virtue."[4] Irony indeed since the Nazi's tried, and partially succeeded, in misinterpreting just about everything he had to say!

Then, there is Walter Benjamin, another German philosopher who said, "First, capitalism is a pure religious cult, perhaps the most extreme there ever was."[5] And, in the Book of Exodus in The Bible, the Golden Calf is depicted as a symbol of idolatry. However, the bronze *Charging Bull,* a piece of art that has become a hugely popular international tourist attraction, is certainly a symbol of Wall Street: financial optimism and greater prosperity."

Of course, what a further irony it is that most wedding rings and halos are golden, and the reward for student achievement has historically been a gold star.

Plate 8
John A. O'Connor, *A Certain "T",* 2016-17. Digital Image, 21 x 17 in.

WHITE LIES MATTER

But you know, you do have a problem because half of the [American] people don't pay any tax.[1]
—Donald Trump

Ironically, 100% die.

This shibboleth, "Nothing is certain except for death and taxes" is attributed by some sources to Benjamin Franklin—while others say it belongs to Mark Twain or Daniel Defoe.

Benjamin Franklin, who wrote in a 1789 letter that "Our new Constitution is now established, and has an appearance that promises permanency; but in this world nothing can be said to be certain, except death and taxes."[2] However, *The Yale Book of Quotations* includes the following statement from Christopher Bullock, The Cobler of Preston (1716), "Tis impossible to be sure of any thing but Death and Taxes." The same source also includes the quote, "Death and Taxes, they are certain," from Edward Ward, The Dancing Devils (1724).[3]

The "business card" in this "slate" contains a silhouette portrait of Franklin along with the abovementioned quote that is attributed to him. The green line, a "V," represents the wealthiest 1% of the American population, and that idea is reinforced by the repetition of 1% on the bottom border on the "slates frame." Numerous images representing Texas and the "Western Culture" are included in the vertical frame borders as visual puns on the phrase "death and taxes."

The idea of death and taxes also refers to the famous quote "you can't take it with you" the title of a 1936 play by Moss Hart and George S. Kaufman.[4] But, contrary to most popular thinking, a version of the phrase can be found in the Bible. (Check out 1 Timothy 6:7.)

It is also a reference to the so-called "death tax" also known as the estate or inheritance tax. There is so much "gibberish" and misleading information about these taxes that they have earned a place in *White Lies Matter.*

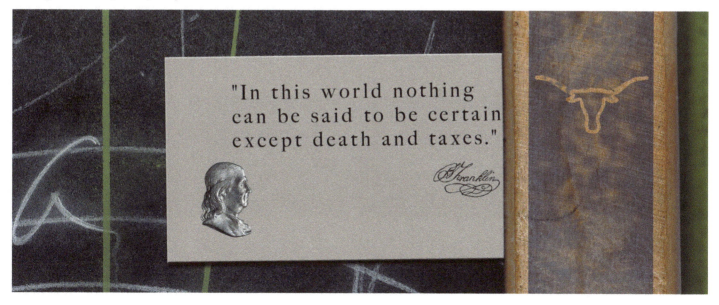

Plate 9
John A. O'Connor, *USAUSAUSA,* 2016-17. Digital Image, 21 x 17 in.

WHITE LIES MATTER

"So long as patriotism dwells among us, so long will this song be the theme of our nation."[1]

Francis Scott Key wrote America's national anthem while he watched the 1814 Battle of Baltimore from a ship in the harbor. Originally a poem titled "Defense of Fort M'Henry,"[2] it was rewritten several times and also then renamed the "The Star Spangled Banner." The "bomb bursting in air" is from the original version. He later changed it to "bombs" bursting in air.

While most Americans assume that it has been our national anthem from the time it was written, it didn't officially became the national anthem until 1931.

Recognized as one of American's most patriotic symbols, it embodied a number of contradictions from the beginning. Written by a person opposed to the war, and also a slave owner, it honors "the land of the free."

And, what of "the home of the brave?" What about the Native Americans? Romanticizing American outlaws? The KKK? And, what do you really know about Teddy Roosevelt and the Rough Riders?

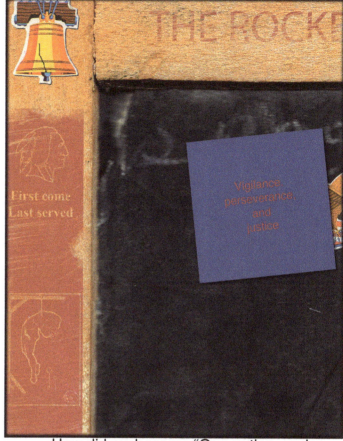

How did we become "One nation, under God?" Why do we have the largest prison population in the world?[3]

How does The Patriot Act preserve our freedoms? Hint: It's not about Tom Brady and his football team?

Why are United States Government officials sworn in on the Bible?

When did women get voting rights?

Are you ready, really ready, to tolerate LGBTQ, and what about their rights?

What's the NDAA?

Do you know what due process really means?

Do you remember Vietnam? The Vietnam War? Do you know that it is not included, in any detail, in most U.S. history textbooks? And, if it is, does it talk about the My Lai Massacre? Or Kent State?[4]

Have you ever heard of the Scopes Monkey Trial?

Well, it's all here for you to decipher!

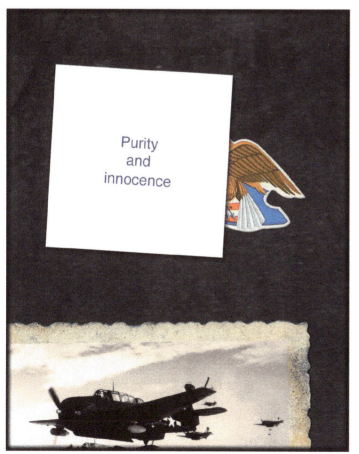

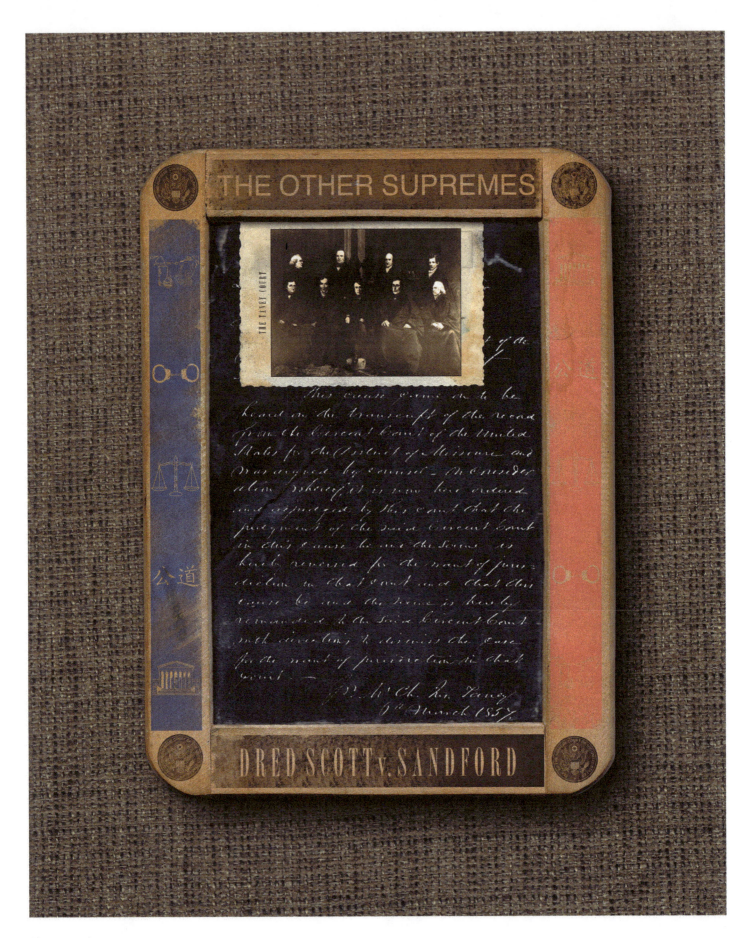

Plate 10
John A. O'Connor, *The Other Supremes,* 2016-17. Digital Image, 21 x 17 in.

WHITE LIES MATTER

"Dred Scott v. Sandford (1857) stands first in any list of the worst Supreme Court decisions—Chief Justice Hughes called it the Court's greatest self-inflicted wound."[1]

What an irony it is that The Supremes were among the greatest and most successful vocal groups of all time—and are listed as "to date America's most successful vocal group."[2]

Isn't that a great paradox that The Supremes chose the name usually reserved for the justices of America's highest court—that same court that gave us the Dred Scott decision?

Dred Scott was an African American who was born in Virginia in 1795 as a slave. His life was a crazy mixture of normality and insanity—apparently quite usual for a black man of that era.

Scott eventually entered a lengthy period seeking his freedom—first by purchasing it for himself and his family (which was not successful), and then, subsequently, through the court system. Thus began a bizarre series of events and even more outlandish trials beginning in 1846—even though by law he apparently had unknowingly already achieved his freedom by marriage in the Wisconsin Territory in 1836 since slavery, supposedly, was already prohibited there.

After another trial in Missouri in 1854, the U.S. Supreme Court received the case and it immediately made its first error–mistakenly misnaming it Dred Scott v. Sandford, the name the case has been known by ever since. (The man Scott sued was named John **Sanford**.)[3]

To add even more absurdity to this case, in fact to make it seem even more contemporary, it was discovered that then-President-elect James Buchanan intervened illegally in the case by pressuring two of the justices. In its decision, the Supreme Court of the United States of America ruled that Scott was not an American citizen—and therefore he had no legal right to sue for his freedom! Not only did Scott have no legal right to sue for his freedom, Chief Justice Roger Taney wrote extensively about how neither slaves nor their descendents were people. Then, he continued on about how the Declaration of Independence made that quite clear. He sustained his lengthy commentary in order to make it absolutely clear that, in his opinion, the Constitution of the United States specifically spells out the right of Americans to import slaves and to own them. The decision also concluded that the Fifth Amendment to the U.S. Constitution (what is referred to today as "pleading the fifth" when one does not wish to incriminate oneself) actually protected slaveholder's rights.[4]

Two of the Supreme Court justices did dissent from the majority decision. Democrats, such as they were at that period in our history, generally applauded the decision, while most Republicans denounced it.

And then, even more ironically, Scott's ownership was transferred again so that his former owner's husband, a staunch abolitionist, could avoid being justly labeled a hypocrite. Eighteen months before Dred Scott's death, he was freed.

Plate 11
John A. O'Connor, *Women's Suffrage,* 2017. Digital Image, 21 x 17 in.

WHITE LIES MATTER

"Had the suffrage movement not been so ignored by historians, women like Lucretia Mott, Carrie Chapman Catt and Alice Paul would be as familiar to most Americans as Thomas Jefferson, Theodore Roosevelt or Martin Luther King, Jr. We would know the story of how women were denied the right to vote despite the lofty words of the Constitution, how women were betrayed after the Civil War, defeated and often cheated in election after election, and how they were forced to fight for their rights against entrenched opposition with virtually no financial, legal or political power."[1]

On August 18, 1920—when the 19th Amendment to the United States Constitution was ratified—American women finally gained voting equality with black men. Black men supposedly had achieved voting equality with white men in 1870 when the 15th Amendment to the United States Constitution was passed. It took a mere 70 years from the origination of the women's rights movement to achieve that goal.[2]

What is perhaps less well known is that Democrat President Woodrow Wilson opposed women's right to vote. During his inauguration in 1913, many women suffragettes were injured as they paraded through the streets of Washington, D. C. in support of their cause.[3]

By 1918, Wilson decided to switch his position on voting rights for women apparently because of the role women had played in World War I. However, even with the president's support, the amendment failed in the Senate. In 1919, the House and Senate passed the amendment, then sent it to the states for ratification. After thirty five states had ratified the amendment, it was up to a twenty three-year-old Republican from McMinn County in Tennessee. Harry T. Burn, in an unusual reversal of his position opposing the amendment that supposedly came about at the urging of his mother, cast the deciding vote for approval. With that vote and certification on August 26, 1920, the 19th Amendment was official. Almost sixty four years later, Mississippi finally ratified it in—a typically Orwellian twist—1984.

Ironically, Wyoming, now recognized as the most conservative state,[4] approved women's suffrage in 1869 and elected its first woman to statewide office in 1894.[5] But the first state to elect any woman to statewide office was North Dakota. It elected Laura Eisenhuth, a Democrat, to the office of Superintendent of Public Instruction in 1892.[6]

It is very interesting to note that the two states currently listed as the most conservative in America were the first to elect statewide female

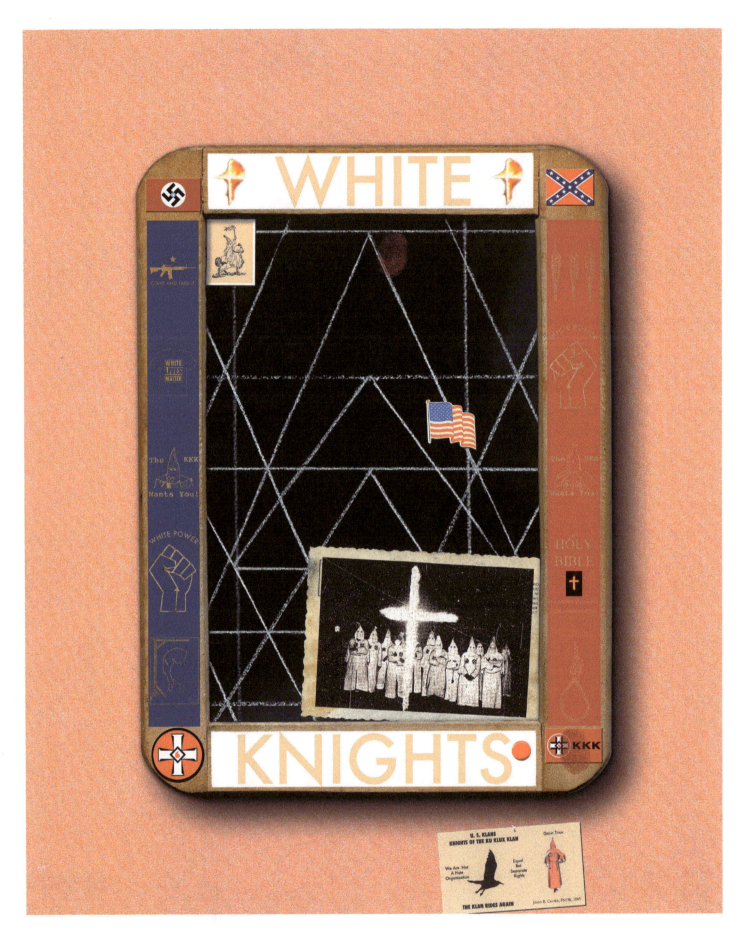

Plate 12
John A. O'Connor, *White Knights,* 2018. Digital Image, 21 x 17 in.

WHITE LIES MATTER

What is the Ku Klux Klan? When was it founded? Was the Klan the result of the Civil War?

A Christian organization that attacked blacks, Jews, gays, people from other countries—and even Catholics, it has had exalted Cyclops, Imperial Wizards, and Grand Dragons and utilized tar and featherings and rape as its greeting card—a "hallmark of the Klan."[1]

"The Ku Klux Klan is now the oldest single-purpose terrorist organization in the world maintaining the same title and focus."[2] Ironically, one of its initial founders was named James R. Crowe.

In 2017, the KKK is an active, widespread group of people located in California, Delaware, Florida, New York, Illinois, Indiana, Maine, Michigan, New Jersey, New York, Ohio, Pennsylvania, and Washington—as well as all over the South.[3]

"When Trump buoyed the Ku Klux Klan and the neo-Nazis who had marched in Charlottesville with Tiki torches, Confederate flags, Nazi slogans, swastikas and banners reading 'Jews will not replace us'—even as one of their leaders told a Vice News reporter how disgusting it was that Trump's 'beautiful' blond daughter was married to a Jewish man—the president made it clear which category he is in."[4]

But, before we blame Trump, Republicans, and the Alt-Right, let's take a hard look at the Southern Democrats following the Civil War. Formed in Tennessee in 1865, the KKK was a social club for former soldiers of the confederacy, but it soon evolved into a group of activists opposed to Republican political power and Southern blacks.[5]

There seem to be innumerable theories about why they named the group the Ku Klux Klan. One reliable source suggests that Ku Klux was derived from the Greek word "kyklos" which is translated as "circle" and the word "klan" is a variation on the Gaelic word for a "clan."[6]

Hmm. So, the Confederate soldiers who formed this group were conversant in Greek? Or, perhaps the origin of the phrase is the sound of cocking a rifle? Some sources attribute its origin to the latter—invoking Sherlock Holmes in the Sir Arthur Conan Doyle story, "Five Orange Pips." But, since this story wasn't published until 1891, how could that be the source—unless the Confederate soldiers had glimpsed the future?[7] After all, their garb—white hoods and robes—were symbols of their ghostly, unearthly nature.[8]

By the 1940s, the Klan, following its efforts "to create a more stable social order," had become opposed to labor unions and Communism "claiming the Klan was the only 'all-American patriotic, fraternal, and political movement in the U.S."[9]

And a final thought: Don't they sound just like all of the fiercely patriotic Americans of today?

Plate 13

John A. O'Connor, *Redacted,* 2016-17. Digital Image, 21 x 17 in.

WHITE LIES MATTER

As the Anthony Comstocks of today patrol the Halls of this Congress seeking to suppress free speech and reproductive choice in the name of morality, or family values, or whatever high-sounding purpose they may invoke, it is incumbent upon the Congress to ensure that no form of the Comstock Act is ever again enacted, and that no special agent is ever again commissioned to roam the land, persecuting Americans in the name of morality or family values.

—Patricia Schroeder, September 24, 1996—U.S. House of Representatives, Washington, DC

Who is this handsome nineteenth century rogue? Well, he was an American, a Victorian, a Civil War veteran, and an active member of the Young Men's Christian Association.

He was also a U.S. Postal Service Inspector who is probably best remembered for creating the New York Society for the Suppression of Vice in 1873–the same year he convinced Congress to pass the law named after him.

So what law was that? Well, it was called the Comstock Law, and it had far reaching consequences for people of his time, and for people of our time. (A protege of his was no less than J. Edgar Hoover.) The law made it illegal to deliver by mail or any other method of transportation "obscene, lewd, or lascivious" material. It also prohibited the production or publication of any material that related to abortion, birth control, or even preventing STDs.

In 1895, the *New York Times* came up with the term "comstockery" to denote "censorship because of perceived obscenity or immorality." George Bernard Shaw (Irish playwright, Nobel Prize and Academy Award winner, and author of more than sixty plays) tangled with Comstock

John A. O'Connor, **Anthony Comstock,** 2012, Charcoal on Paper, 9 x 6 in.

over his play *Mrs. Warren's Profession* and said, "Comstockery is the world's standing joke at the expense of the United States," and went on to proclaim that it proved to Europeans that America was a second-rate, provincial country.[3] So what is the status of the Comstock Act in America in 2018. "The law that bears his name continues on the books, although gradually weakened and largely unenforced."[4]

This grand gentleman most certainly would have had an elegant and dignified business card.

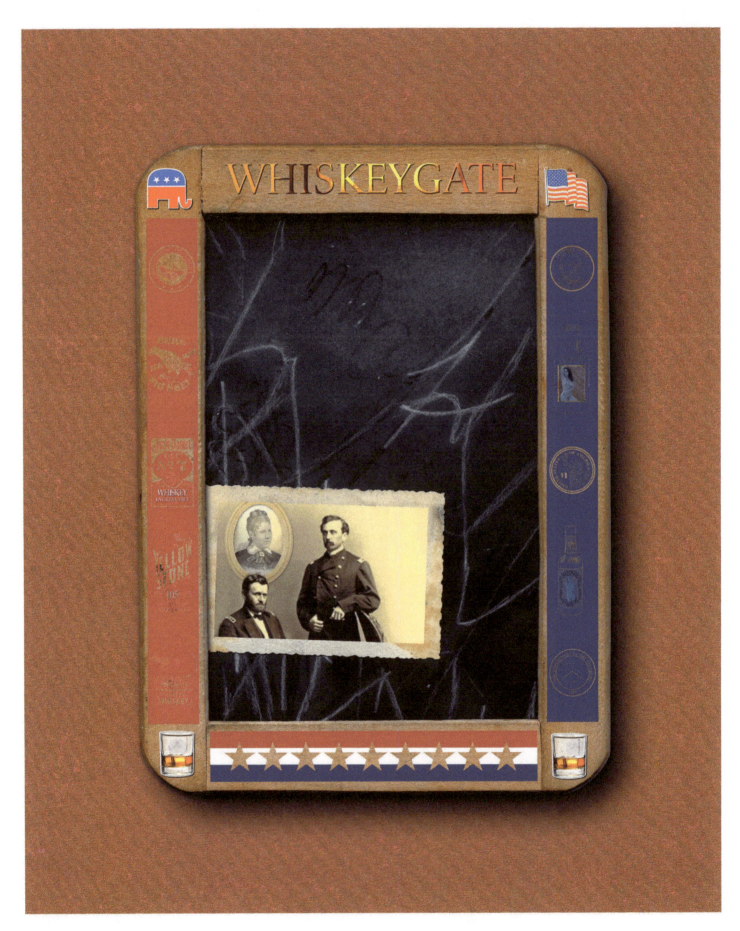

Plate 14

John A. O'Connor, *Whiskeygate,* 2018. Digital Image, 21 x 17 in.

"As long as you're up, get me a Grant's" dates to the 1950s.[1] But the Whiskey Ring Scandal dates back to its formation in 1871. Ingenuously designed to raise funds for Republican politicians who backed then-President Grant's re-election effort, it was a huge success. According to Grant's U.S. Attorney David P. Dyer,

> They kept an account at the distillers of all the illicit whisky that was made, and the gaugers and store-keepers were paid from one to two dollars for each barrel that was turned out . . . and every Saturday reported to the collector of the ring the amount of crooked whisky, and either the distiller or the gauger paid the money over as the case might be. The arrangement between distiller and rectifier was that thirty-five cents . . . was divided between him and the rectifier. That division was made by the distiller selling crooked whisky . . . at seventeen cents a gallon less than the market-price. That is how the rectifier got his share of the amount retained by the distiller. The amount paid to the officers was on each Saturday evening taken to the office of the supervisor of internal revenue and there divided . . . and distributed among them.[2]

Participants in this great American venture received up to $60,000 in one year—or more than $1.05 million in 2016 dollars.[3] And, by 1873, this group of Republicans was siphoning off at least $1.5 million a year from the U.S. Treasury.[4] But in 1874, following the appointment of Secretary of the Treasury Benjamin Bristow and the subsequent involvement of Myron Colony, Commercial Editor of the *St. Louis Democrat* newspaper and his cohorts, Bristow finally had the information he "needed to arrest the whiskey thieves."[5] (An interesting corollary to this intrigue is that the other leading newspaper there was the

St. Louis Dispatch owned by Joseph Pulitzer whose name would be subsequently associated with the most prestigious award in journalism. Ironically, it is also the name of the man, along with William Randolph Hearst, most associated with "yellow journalism"—yesterday's version of today's "fake news."[6]

By May 1875, the U.S. government had arrested in excess of three hundred whiskey ring conspirators including numerous federal government officials. But by August, President U.S. Grant sensed that General Orville Babcock, his private secretary and most trusted aide's involvement would lead straight to the president himself. Although Grant and Babcock maneuvered through a number of options and legal loopholes, Babcock's trial was set for February 7, 1876.[7]

Through a dizzying array of events, unexpected moves, unprecedented then and now rivaling "anything which Watergate or Iran-Contra have had to offer,"[8] President Grant decided to testify as a witness for the defense of General Babcock. However, Grant's Secretary of State Hamilton Fish convinced the president to provide only a written deposition to a number of questions that both the prosecution and defense had agreed to in advance. Ironically, President Grant's "legendary photographic memory consistently failed him throughout most of the deposition, but it did not fail him when it came to Babcock. The President had no trouble remembering his aide's fidelity and efficiency nor in testifying to his universally good reputation among men of affairs."[9] Ultimately, Babcock was acquitted—the only important Whiskey Ring Scandal defendant so "lucky."

Paradoxically, Babcock was indicted less than two weeks later for another U.S. Grant administration scandal. Although he was acquitted again and subsequently appointed to the position of Chief Inspector of Lighthouses, he reportedly drowned near the well-named Mosquito Inlet, Florida, in 1884.[10]

Plate 15
John A. O'Connor, *A Big Stick,* 2018. Digital Image, 21 x 17 in.

WHITE LIES MATTER

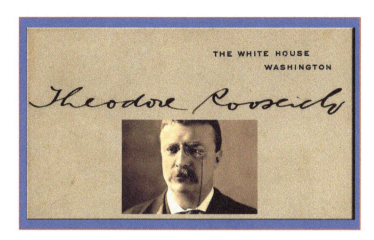

The idea for—and the incredible multitude of problems with—the Panama Canal did not begin with the Americans. There were significant, prior plans, efforts and failures to build a cross-Panama canal primarily by the French (one of which resulted in the prosecution of, among others, Gustave Eiffel, the designer of the famed Eiffel Tower in Paris).[1]

While American interest in a cross-Panama canal began as early as 1826, no successful effort was completed. However, in 1903, following the failure of Colombia to sign a treaty with the U.S. that would have allowed it to complete the failed French attempt, American President Theodore Roosevelt decided to support Panamanian rebels in their effort to break away from Colombia, going so far as utilizing U.S. naval assets to block maritime access to the Colombian troops sent to put down the rebellion.[2]

Interestingly, the man who represented the failed French effort to build the canal, one Philippe Bunau-Varilla wrote the declaration of independence for Panama, its constitution, and [his wife] even designed its flag—all from his residence in the Waldorf Astoria Hotel in New York City. The result of this effort and the subsequent Hay-Bunau-Varilla treaty provided the U.S. with "a grant 'in perpetuity of the use, occupation, and control' of a sixteen kilometer-wide strip of territory and extensions of three nautical miles into the sea from each terminal 'for the construction, maintenance, operation, sanitation, and protec-

tion' of an isthmian canal."[3] So, in effect, the U.S. became the "owner" of Panama as a "de facto protectorate."[4]

Following U.S. acquisition of the "rights" to build the Panama Canal (actually to continue the unfinished French debacle), construction began anew in May 1904. One of the first priorities was to reduce the fatalities that had severely hampered the French effort. Dr. William Crawford Gorgas became the chief sanitary officer in Panama in 1904, and he focused his efforts on eliminating the diseases spread by mosquitoes. Although the Walter Reed Commission had—by 1900—established that mosquitoes transmitted yellow fever and malaria, Gorgas met with significant resistance to his efforts by the Canal Commission's chief engineer, among a number of others to "scientifically established fact."[5] My how times haven't changed.

As work on the canal progressed, President Roosevelt apparently had a change in attitude about this colossal undertaking. From a "political, commercial and military necessity," the canal project had become "a mighty battle involving the national honor. . . ."[6]

When President Roosevelt decided to visit "the ditch" in 1906—becoming the first American president to ever leave the United States during his term in office—his most famous quotable phrase, "Speak softly and carry a big stick" appeared to be fulfilled.

Plate 16

John A. O'Connor, *Normalcy,* 2018. Digital Image, 21 x 17 in.

WHITE LIES MATTER

While most Americans today (March 2018) might not be surprised to learn that our elected government leaders have—occasionally—misbehaved, apparently things were quite different back in the roaring twenties. "The Teapot Dome Scandal of the 1920s shocked Americans by revealing an unprecedented level of greed and corruption within the federal government."[1] In fact, before the Watergate Scandal beginning in 1972 under President Nixon, the "Teapot Dome Scandal was regarded by the public and historians alike as the most sensational example of high-level corruption in the history of U.S. politics."[2]

"Albert Fall, a former Secretary of the Interior, was charged with accepting bribes from oil companies in exchange for exclusive rights to drill for oil on federal land. The sites included land near a teapot-shaped outcrop in Wyoming known as Teapot Dome, and two other government-owned sites in California named Elk Hills and Buena Vista Hills."[3]

There is a great deal of irony here. During the 1920s in the United States, national wealth rose rapidly, large numbers of Americans moved off of farms and into cities, and the public embraced chain stores—thus developing the beginning of a significant, new, large-scale consumer society.[4] A unique American symbol of "woman" appeared: the flapper who drank, smoked, and swore. Radio flourished, phonograph records became popular, movie theaters were visited by most Americans once a week, Henry Ford had already revolutionized the auto industry with his innovative Model T. Jazz became fashionable—although like rock 'n' roll three decades later, it provoked a lot of folks, particularly older ones. Much like many Americans' response to the rock music of the 50s and 60s, many people in the 20s were convinced that jazz provoked vulgar actions and caused people to do depraved things while its adherents loved it for the freedom they believed it brought.[5]

But, during the 1920s, a great number of contradictory things were occurring: while jazz played and the flappers danced and the Model T took off, booze was banned. That's right! With all of this newfound freedom that Americans were beginning to experience, the U.S. government had banned "intoxicating liquors" in 1919. On January 16, 1920, the U.S. government shut down all bars in the United States. Prohibition was the word, order, and rule of the day. But, unlike its intended function "to assert some control over the unruly immigrant masses who crowded the nation's cities,"[6] it had numerous, unintended consequences. Or did it? Did it turn back the clock to a more civil and civilized time where white picket fences surrounded immaculate private residences and women stayed home and raised children? Was that the idea? Was it to "Make America Great Again!"? Ironically, like today, it was accompanied with a skyrocketing jump in the number of white Americans joining the Ku Klux Klan.[7] And, at the same time, America experienced a growing anti-Communist and anti-immigrant fervor. In 1924, American insecurity provided the climate for passage of the National Origins Act that favored immigration by northern Europeans rather than eastern Europeans or Asians.[8] Does that sound familiar? ("We want Norwegians!")

These extraordinary and rapid cultural changes followed the presidential election of 1920 when Warren G. Harding, backed by oil company executives,[9] won the presidency by the largest percentage margin in American history.[10] It was a reaction to all of these changes, exhaustion with World War I, and negative reaction to the proposed League of Nations.

It was, after all, just an American desire for a return to normality—which President Harding described as a return to normalcy: A time of God, guns, and oil, and, of course, those comforting white picket fences.

Plate 17

John A. O'Connor, *That Old Black Magic,* 2016-17. Digital Image, 21 x 17 in.

WHITE LIES MATTER

Drill baby drill.

—Michael Steele, Chairman, Republican National Committee

oil operates 24/7 and disrupts "wildlife, water sources, human health, recreation and other purposes for which public lands were set aside and held in trust for the American people."[3] "Haze, toxic chemicals and dust pollute the air and water. Open pits, ponds, and lagoons can contain wastewater, organic chemicals, petroleum hydrocarbons, surfactants and other substances

"That Old Black Magic"—a popular song first recorded and released as a single by Glenn Miller and His Orchestra—rose to number 8 on the *Billboard Top 100* in 1943[1]

Black magic or dark magic has traditionally referred to the use of supernatural powers or magic for evil and selfish purposes.[2] I use the song lyrics (included in the work as a piece of "wrinkled paper") to describe the opposite condition from what the effects of oil are. In other words, I am using the uplifting song, "That Old Black Magic" as a metaphor for an exactly opposite situation: one that is destructive to the environment.

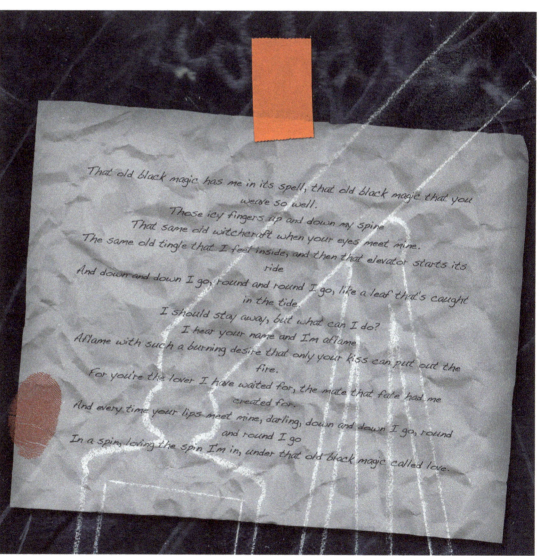

The corporate logos are used in a generic oil drilling company's "business card." There are "bloody fingerprints" that symbolize an entire litany of what can go wrong with drilling for oil. If the viewer looks closely, he/she will notice an oil-drilling rig depicted on the "slate." Drilling for

that compromise the safety of our water. Pipeline explosions and wells (even if properly drilled) can cause drinking-water problems by cross-contaminating aquifers. Development of gas wells may even require releases of methane and myriad toxic gases into the atmosphere.[4]

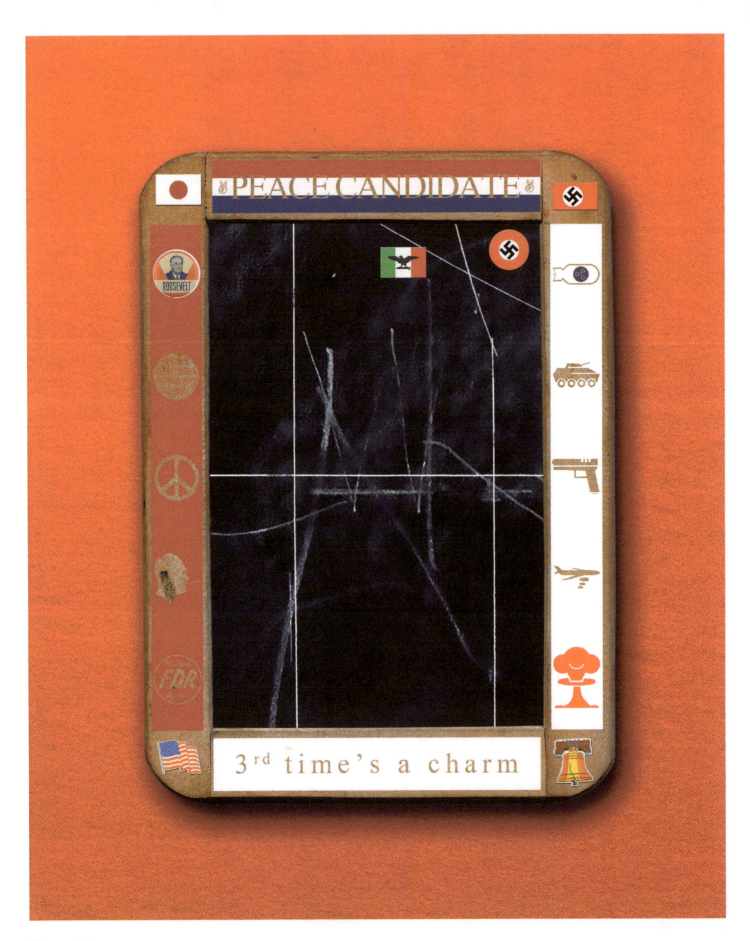

Plate 18

John A. O'Connor, *3rd Time's a Charm,* 2018. Digital Image, 21 x 17 in.

Franklin Delano Roosevelt ran for president for the third time in 1940—thus breaking a long-standing two-term limit that dates back to George Washington. Opposed by some in his own party—including his then-vice president—Roosevelt ran as a "peace candidate" while, at the same time, he called "the U.S. 'an arsenal for democracy.' " Then he signed the Selective Service Act that September.[1]

Hmm. Let's see. A peace candidate with an arsenal for democracy and a peacetime military draft.

On October 28, 1940, Roosevelt then went on to say, "I am asking the American people to support a continuance of this type of affirmative, realistic fight for peace. The alternative is to risk the future of the country in the hands of those with this record of timidity, weakness and short-sightedness or to risk it in the inexperienced hands of those who in these perilous days are willing recklessly to imply that our boys are already on their way to the transports. This affirmative search for peace calls for clear vision. It is necessary to mobilize resources, minds and skills, and every active force for peace in all the world."[2]

Two days later, Roosevelt said, "Time after time, Republican leadership refused to see that what this country needs is an all-American team.

Those side-line critics are now saying that we are not doing enough for our national defense. I say to you that we are going full speed ahead! Our Navy is our outer line of defense.

Almost the very minute that this Administration came into office seven and a half years ago, we began to build the Navy up- to build a bigger Navy.

In those seven years we have raised the total of 193 ships in commission to 337 ships in commission today.

And, in addition to that, we have 19 more ships that are actually under construction today.

In those seven years we raised the personnel of our Navy from 106,000 to 210,000 today."

He continued, saying he had "more than doubled the size of our regular Army." And he went on to note that 800,000 "young men" were being called up in 1940 alone under the Selective Service Act. Then, he added, "General Marshall said to me the other day that the task of training those young men is, for the Army, a 'profound privilege.' "[3]

Roosevelt then informed the American public, "And while I am talking to you mothers and fathers, I give you one more assurance.

I have said this before, but I shall say it again and again and again:

Your boys are not going to be sent into any foreign wars."

One year and a few days later, the U.S. declared war on Japan and then Germany. By the end of World War II, more than 16.1 million Americans had served in the war. Only 292,000 Americans were killed in battle while the total number of deaths was estimated to be 72 million. Almost 2 billion people were directly involved worldwide.[4]

Yes! **Two billion**.

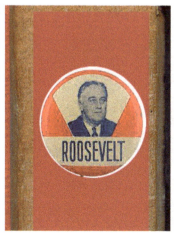

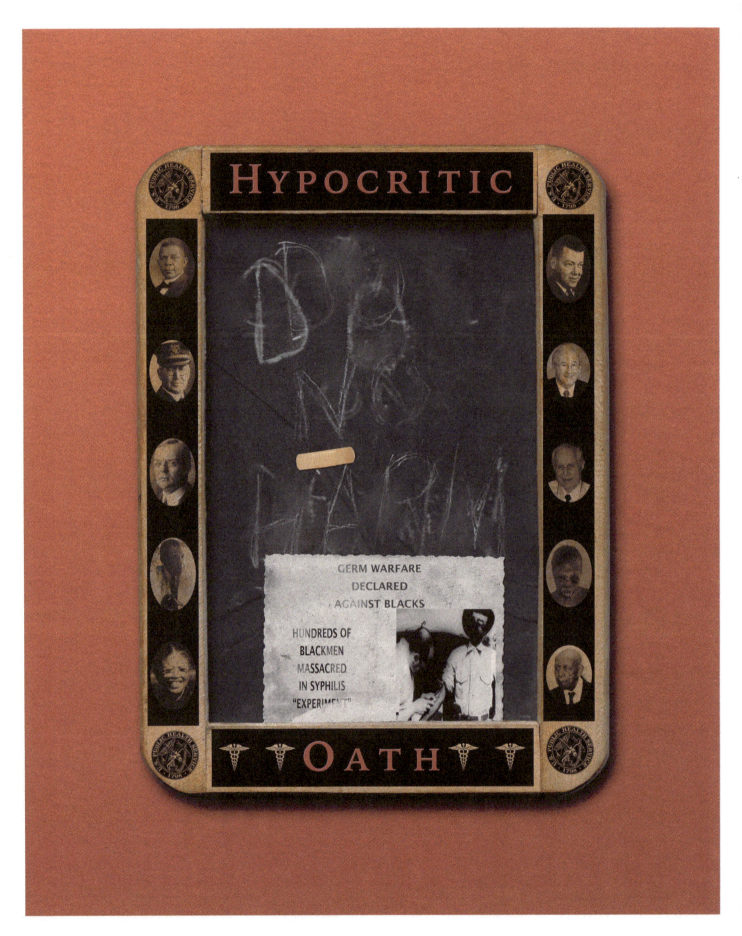

Plate 19

John A. O'Connor, *Hypocritic Oath,* 2018. Digital Image, 21 x 17 in.

GERM WARFARE

DECLARED

AGAINST BLACKS

The United States government and American medicine have an ugly record when it comes to mutual collaboration. Probably the most infamous example of this collusion was the Tuskegee Syphilis Experiment—officially known as the Tuskegee Study of Untreated Syphilis in the Negro Male.

This remarkable episode in American medical practice was designed to last six months,[1] but it went on for forty years! Not exposed until June 1972 by Jean Heller of the Associated Press, this so-called "study" was conducted by the United States Public Health Service to study the effects of untreated syphilis on black men[2] in partnership with the Tuskegee Institute, (now Tuskegee University) a historically black university founded by Booker T. Washington. At least 600 poor, black men were in this study, with approximately two-thirds of them already infected with syphilis. They were never informed that they had the disease, but rather they were told that they had "bad blood."[3]

The sole constant in this experiment was a black nurse, Eunice Rivers, who was involved from the beginning until the end. In fact, her role with the infected men became one of a coordinator who morphed into a very peculiar structure: she became the symbol and embodiment of "Miss Rivers' Lodge,"—"a social club and burial society. . . ."

"Black doctors, nurses, and even the President of Tuskegee Institute, either participated in, endorsed or encouraged the study—apparently because they believed in it. However, it was a white woman doctor named Anne R. Yobs who blocked the initial disclosure of this study by Dr. Irwin Schatz. Dr. Schatz had written the U.S. Public Health Service in 1965, 'I am ut-

terly astounded by the fact that physicians allow patients with a potentially fatal disease to remain untreated when effective therapy is available. I assume you feel that the information which is extracted from observation of this untreated group is worth their sacrifice. If this is the case, then I suggest the United States Public Health Service and those physicians associated with it in this study need to re-evaluate their moral judgments in this regard.' " Schatz's letter was addressed to a Dr. Donald H. Rockwell who passed it on to Dr. Yobs.[4]

"This American example of racially based medical experimenting began in 1932 before the Germans began their experiments on Jews, homosexuals, and other groups during the Holocaust."[5]

It wasn't until 1997 that this terrible epoch in American medical ethics came to some conclusion. President Clinton apologized for this loathsome malpractice, and in 1999, the Tuskegee University Center for Bioethics was created.[6]

But the Tuskegee Study was not the only example of appalling American medical practices that were as reprehensible as those of the Nazis before and during World War II. From 1946-48, the U.S. Public Health Service also conducted a sexually transmitted disease study on unknowing people in Guatemala. Ironically, perhaps, this study, the "U.S. PUBLIC HEALTH SERVICE SEXUALLY TRANSMITTED DISEASES INOCULATION STUDY OF 1946-48" was recorded by a Dr. John Cutler who had also been involved in the Tuskegee Study.[7]

The good news, if you believe it, is that, "Such abuses could not occur today in research funded or conducted by the U.S. government."[8]

Plate 20
John A. O'Connor, *Interment? Internment!,* 2018. Digital Image, 21 x 17 in.

WHITE LIES MATTER

Interment
Interment took place in the churchyard.
—Oxford English Dictionary

Internment
He was threatened with internment in a concentration camp.
—Oxford English Dictionary

On February 19, 1942, U.S. President Franklin Roosevelt, signed Executive Order 9066 that authorized the government to remove Japanese men, women and children—whether alien or American citizens—from any area designated by the Secretary of War. It also provided that the people removed would be provided "transportation, food, shelter, and other accommodations as may be necessary. . . ."[1]

"Major Karl Bendetsen and Lieutenant General John L. DeWitt, head of the Western Command, each questioned Japanese American loyalty. DeWitt, who administered the internment program, repeatedly told newspapers that 'A Jap's a Jap' and testified to Congress, I don't want any of them [persons of Japanese ancestry] here. They are a dangerous element. There is no way to determine their loyalty. . . It makes no difference whether he is an American citizen, he is still a Japanese. American citizenship does not necessarily determine loyalty. . . But we must worry about the Japanese all the time until he is wiped off the map."[2]

The U.S. government authorized detention camps to provide the forced removal of more than 120,000 Japanese—of whom 80,000 were American citizens. But where was the relocation of German- and Italian-Americans? After all, we were at war with Germany and Italy as well as Japan?

Earl Warren, Attorney General of California at the time of Roosevelt's Executive Order 9066, was frequently chastised by conservative Republicans for being too progressive. Warren, however, really was "all over the ballpark." He once prosecuted a woman for attending a communist meeting, was a member of the secret society at the University of California, Berkeley, known as "The Gun Club," and rose to the level of Grand Master in the Freemasons in California.[3]

In developing the executive order to "relocate" the Japanese living in the U.S., three military leaders and Warren were the chief supporters of this program. Warren would, subsequently in his memoirs, state that he "deeply regretted the removal order and my testimony advocating it because it was not in keeping with our American concept of freedom and the rights of citizens." But before he said that, he already had said, "If the Japs are released no one will be able to tell a saboteur from any other Jap. . . . We don't want to have a second Pearl Harbor in California. We don't propose to have the Japs back in California during this war if there is any lawful means of preventing it."[4]

Japanese-American, Fred Korematsu refused to obey Executive Order 9066, had plastic surgery to alter his appearance, and changed his name. But in May 1942, he was arrested for not reporting to a "relocation center." He was convicted for violating military orders, but his attorneys appealed his case all the way up to the United States Supreme Court. On December 18, 1944, the Supreme Court upheld his conviction on a 6-3 ruling. And, astonishingly, it held that the decision was "not based on race."[5]

Almost forty years later, the case was re-opened based on "government misconduct." Documents existed showing that Japanese-Americans "posed no military threat to the U.S." On November 10, 1983, Korematsu's conviction was overturned, ironically, in the same courthouse in San Francisco where he had been convicted.[6]

Finally! A victory! Right? Well, not quite. The U.S. Supreme Court decision still stands. Yes, a district court cleared his name, but the highest court did not. In fact, the highest court's original decision has been characterized as "the legalization of racism."[7]

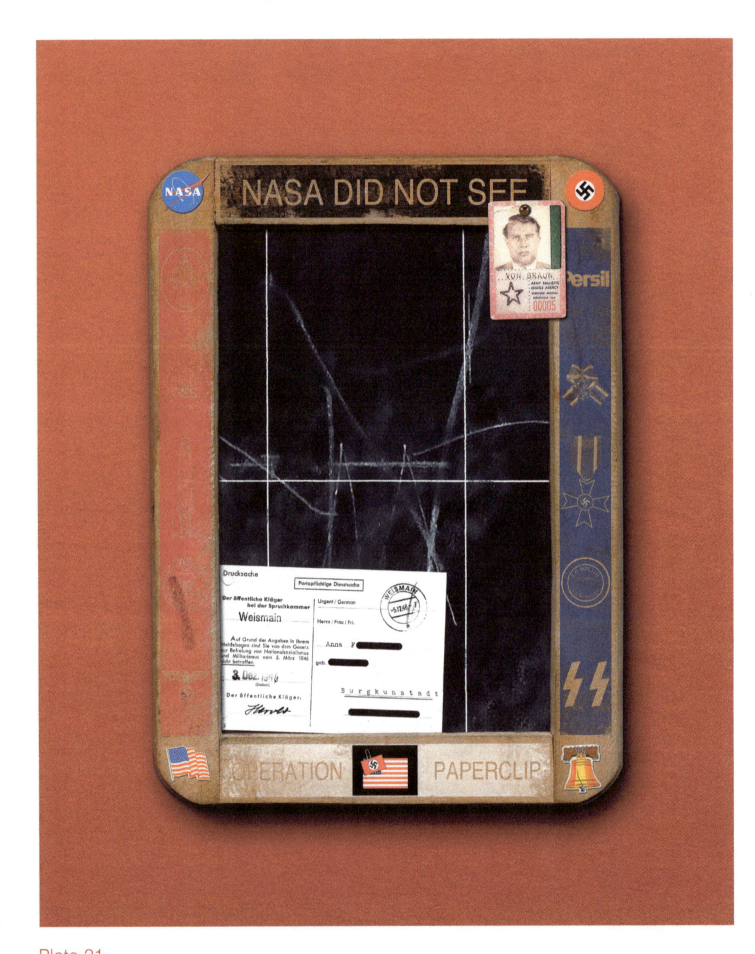

Plate 21

John A. O'Connor, *NASA'S Nazis,* 2016-17. Digital Image, 21 x 17 in.

WHITE LIES MATTER

"Among the trophies of the Second World War captured by Allied intelligence agents were Nazi scientists and their research on biological and chemical weapons."[1]

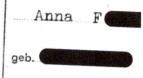

Auf Grund der Angaben in Ihrem Meldebogen sind Sie von dem Gesetz ur Befreiung von Nationalsozialismus nd Militarismus vom 5. März 1946 icht betroffen.

Anna F

geb.

At the end of World War II, most Americans were euphoric. National Socialism (better known by most of us as Fascism) had been defeated. Families were reunited. Victory celebrations went on for days. Was this really the beginning of a new era brought about by the real "War to end all Wars," or was it the beginning of the nuclear age?

As the world returned to normal, behind the scenes Russian, British, and American government officials (and others) rushed to claim the German scientists who created the ideas and weapons that almost propelled the Fascist coalition to victory. In the United States, the War Department dubbed that program Operation Overcast. Eventually renamed Operation Paperclip, this program was approved by President Truman in September 1946—although it excluded German scientists known "to have been a member of the Nazi party and more than a nominal participant in its activities, or an active supporter of Naziism or militarism."[2]

Well, guess what? Apparently, it turned out that all of the first group of scientists were "ardent Nazis,"[3] and they were all rejected by the Department of State and Department of Justice. The designated agency responsible for this operation was called JIOA—Joint Intelligence Objectives Agency, and its director was outraged—furious enough to declare that "the best interests of the United States have been subjugated to the efforts expended in '**beating a dead Nazi horse.**' "[4] [Emphasis added.]

It was subsequently learned that the U.S. Central Intelligence Agency, in cooperation with a former Nazi spy, rewrote all of the scientists' records. By the second year of the Eisenhower ad-

ministration, at least 760 German scientists who had committed war crimes were granted U.S. citizenship. There were no cries then to "build a wall."

Werner von Braun, featured in the slate *NASA's Nazis,* was one of these scientists. Eventually, von Braun would become the associate administrator of NASA, our National Aeronautics and Space Administration. Von Braun had formerly been director of the German rocket center that developed the V-2 rocket that devastated England in World War II.[5]

Other scientists approved by the U.S. government included those who had directed Nazi concentration camps and developed biological and chemical warfare materials such as plague vaccines.

No one can ever be certain how many German scientists and their families came to the United States following World War II, but it appears that the conservative estimate is at least 5,000.

Plate 22

John A. O'Connor, *Alienatiion,* 2018. Digital Image, 21 x 17 in.

WHITE LIES MATTER

The Roswell Incident occurred in July 1947 when a UFO (Unidentified Flying Object) crashed (apparently) somewhere on a ranch near Roswell, New Mexico. First-hand reports from the site at that time were made by a rancher named "Mack" Brazel who described unusual metal fragments spread over a significantly large area and a several hundred foot long trench cut into the ground. When Mack showed some of the objects to his neighbors, they suggested it might be from an alien space vessel and should be reported to the sheriff.[1] (They always tell you to report these things to the sheriff!)

Well, so the story goes, Mack dutifully did report this incident to the sheriff who then reported it to the 509th Bomb Squad officer who was stationed at the Roswell Army Air Field (RAAF). Then, on July 8, a RAAF public information officer wrote a press release in which he described the recovery of material from a disc-like object that had crashed. But, later that same day, the press release was vacated, and the wreckage that had been found had (apparently) been replaced with a weather balloon. The debris that had been recovered had mysteriously vanished.[2]

Then, a week or so later, after a number of military and other personnel had been involved in this "investigation," Mack Brazel changed his story—claiming to have found the debris a week later than he had earlier reported and that he had found weather balloon debris before.

The other obvious question is what is the connection with the Roswell Incident and Area 51? The origination of this top-secret military base in a desolate, uninhabited southern Nevada desert, and reputedly where remnants of the Roswell Incident were taken, correlates with the infamous U-2 spy plane development.[3] The alien lore area has also made this part of southern Nevada a big tourist destination. There is "The Extraterrestrial Highway"—the name given to Nevada State Route 375 in 1996. And, there is the Little A'Le'Inn (Alien) a bar/restaurant in Rachel.[4] There is also the Alien Cathouse west of Area 51—an alien-themed whorehouse.

The Roswell Incident prompted the U.S. government to begin inquiries into UFOs in 1948. Later known as "Project Blue Book" (how appropriate: just like the small bluebooks used for university tests), it eventually investigated 12,618 so-called "close encounters" of UFOs, but it shut down its "investigation" in 1969 after finding no evidence of "extraterrestrial vehicles." Yet, apparently 701 of their cases were never explained.[5]

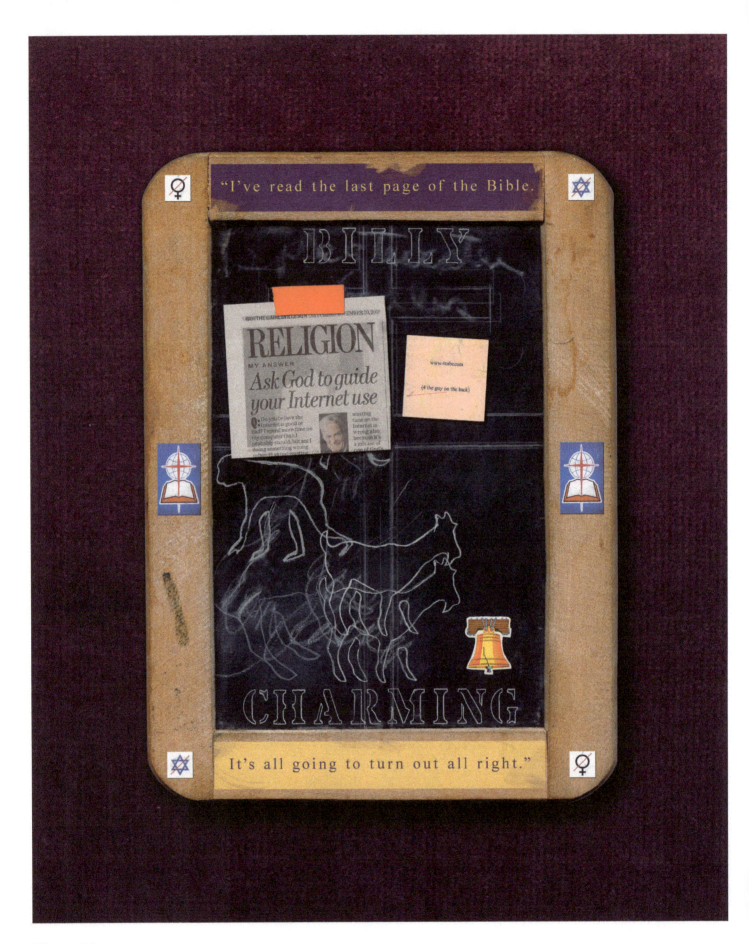

Plate 23

John A. O'Connor, *Charming Billy,* 2016-17. Digital Image, 21 x 17 in.

WHITE LIES MATTER

Charming! Really?

Have you ever heard or read about his comments on women? On Jews? Or on Jews and pornography? What about JFK?

Billy Graham was an internationally known and highly respected Southern Baptist Christian minister who held anti-feminist and anti-Jewish beliefs.

First, there is the "Billy Graham Rule." Named after Billy Graham, the most notable proponent of the practice, it has been adopted as a display of integrity and a means of avoiding sexual temptation,[1] but it also has been criticized as being sexist—even by Christians![2]

Graham called Jews "satanic" and said they had "total domination of the media." And that Jews, "They're the ones putting out the pornographic stuff."[3]

Ironically, Graham's views appear to many to be at odds with Creationist's views on evolution[4]—probably because he graduated from Wheaton College in Illinois in 1943 with **a degree in anthropology!**

Many people have said—some quite sarcastically—that Billy Graham knew everything. It was also said that he could even provide up-to-the-minute advice on how to use the internet—and especially how not to use it. Look very, very closely at the "newspaper clipping" particularly its "backside that is ghosting through, and also the "post-it" note to see what I mean.

The Southern Baptist Convention finally voted in 1995 to adopt a resolution renouncing its racist roots and apologizing for its past defense of slavery, segregation, and white supremacy. However, women still are not eligible to serve as pastors.[5]

The Billy Graham Center archives the records of the Fellowship Foundation–Collection 459. The Fellowship was founded in 1935 in opposition to FDR's New Deal. Dwight D. Eisenhower was the first U.S. president to attend.[5] Jeff Sharlet stated in an NBC Nightly News report that when he was an intern with the Fellowship "we were being taught the leadership lessons of Hitler, Lenin and Mao."[6]

Graham was repeatedly on Gallup's list of most admired men and women appearing 60 times since 1955—more than any other individual in the world.

Graham "is a lifelong registered Democrat,"[7] but he opposed John Kennedy for President of the United States because he, along with Norman Vincent Peale and many others, feared that as a Catholic, Kennedy would be indebted to the Pope.[8]

While Billy Graham was also extremely outspoken against communism, and he supported American Cold War policy, he also visited North Korea and its leader Kim Il Sung on two occasions and exchanged gifts with Kim Jong-Il.[9]

Plate 24

John A. O'Connor, *The Original Pledge,* 2016-18. Digital Image, 21 x 17 in.

WHITE LIES MATTER

"I pledge allegiance to my Flag and the Republic for which it stands, one nation, indivisible, with liberty and justice for all."[1]

Jacques-Louis David, *Oath of the Horatii,* 1784, oil on canvas [detail], 129.8 x 167.2 in, Louvre, Paris.

From its origin in 1892 when it was authored by Christian Socialist and Baptist minister Francis Bellamy of Rome, New York, the U.S. Pledge of Allegiance has had a rather complicated and convoluted history. Some equate it and the "Bellamy salute" with Hitler and the Nazis. Others contend that the Hitler salute really is the Roman salute— even if no art or literature from Roman times seems to support that theory. How ironic that the apparent source for this salute is none other than French artist Jacques-Louis David whose *Oath of the Horatii* appears to be the first depiction of this gesture?

The painting by David is far more complex than what it appears to suggest: three men expressing loyalty. As an expression of patriotism, this work embodies three men taking an extreme pledge.

So, what does this have to do with this slate, *The Original Pledge?* Well, the original U.S. pledge of allegiance was very simple, and it was intended to be recited in fifteen seconds or less.

However, it has been changed, added to, and manipulated numerous time. So this slate depicting its changes reveals its references to Jacques Louis David, Rome, fasces, Hitler, and more. In other words, it, like David's painting, is far more complex than it appears to be.

"Under God" was added to the original, changed, version of the pledge in 1954, partly as a slap at so-called godless communism.[2]

This slate contains many symbols. Can you tell what they are? Why do you think that I have included them along with the Pledge of Allegiance?

HINDU HISPANIC JEW LESBIAN
MUSLIM SOCIALIST TAOIST WICCAN

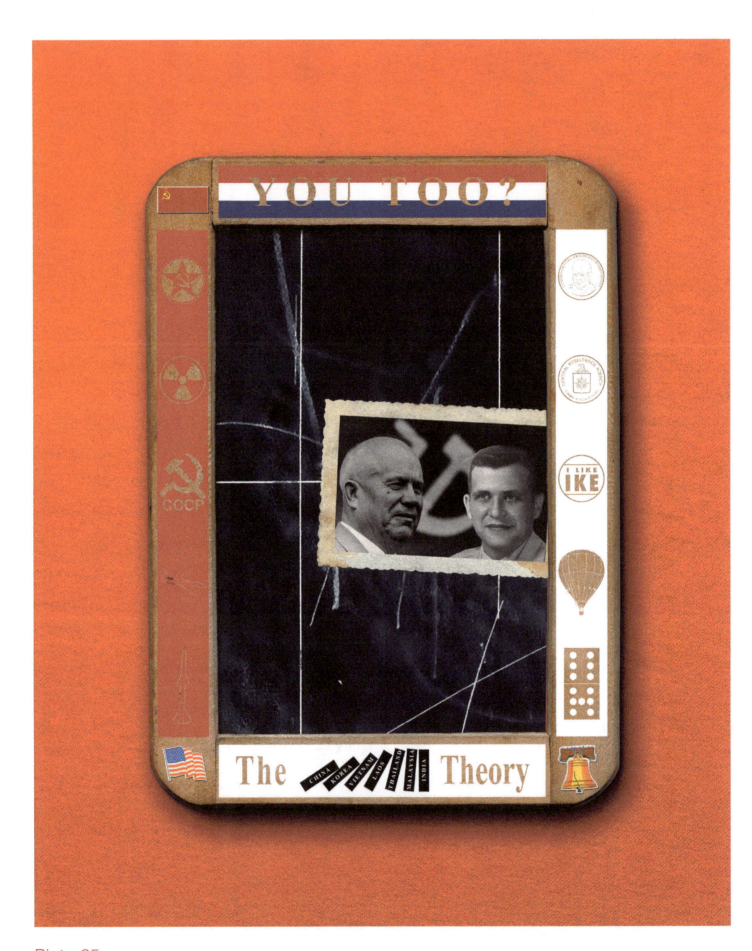

Plate 25
John A. O'Connor, *You Too?,* 2018. Digital Image, 21 x 17 in.

The ~~CHINA KOREA VIETNAM LAOS THAILAND MALAYSIA INDIA~~ Theory

During the Cold War (1945-91), most Americans thought that our archenemy—the USSR—was a belligerent, rogue nation rushing to subjugate its neighbors into submission. The Domino Theory was on almost everyone's lips. Communists were everywhere. We had to do something about it. And, of course, we had been—for quite a while.

President Dwight David Eisenhower, the 34th president of the United States, had approved CIA (U.S. Central Intelligence Agency) spy flights over the Soviet Union. The first "spy flight" occurred on July 4, 1956[1]—ironically as Americans celebrated Independence Day!

Apparently, Eisenhower was very pleased with this method of gathering information on Soviet military technology and facilities, for he was able to ascertain that, rather than lagging behind Soviet nuclear missile production, the U. S. actually had a superior nuclear force.[2]

So, why did the Soviets allow such illegal flights? Flying at 70,000 feet, the American U-2 was able to avoid both Soviet airplanes and missiles—until May 1, 1960. On that date, the U.S. pilot, Francis Gary Powers, was on a secret mission that started in Pakistan and was supposed to end in Norway. Unfortunately for Powers and Eisenhower and the U.S., the USSR had, by then, developed a missile with a far greater range than their previous missiles. The first missile's explosion caused Powers' plane to lose altitude and the second hit the plane directly. Powers managed to bail out. Unfortunately for him, Eisenhower, and the U.S., he landed in the Soviet Union and was captured by the Soviet military.[3]

The Soviets did not mention the incident until five days later and did not hint that they had captured the pilot. Taking the bait, the Eisenhower administration casually confirmed that one of our "weather planes" had accidentally, not intentionally, somehow flown off its intended course.

Soviet leader Khrushchev then revealed on May 7, 1960, that they had captured the American pilot and significant remnants of a spy plane (not a weather plane).[4]

Suddenly the United States of America was thrust into one of the most significant diplomatic scandals of that time. The Soviets wanted an apology from the Americans, but Eisenhower initially refused. By the time Eisenhower changed his mind and admitted that the spy flights had occurred for years and that they would continue, the Soviet Union walked away from the Paris Summit scheduled for May 14. That summit was envisioned as an opportunity for the USSR, France, the UK, and the U.S. to achieve substantial progress and possibly new agreements limiting nuclear testing and production.[5]

And, what of Powers? He was tried, convicted, and sentenced to ten years in a Soviet prison on charges of espionage. Serving less than two years, he was released in 1962 when he was traded for a Soviet agent—apparently the first (acknowledged) "spy swap" between the U.S. and the USSR.[6]

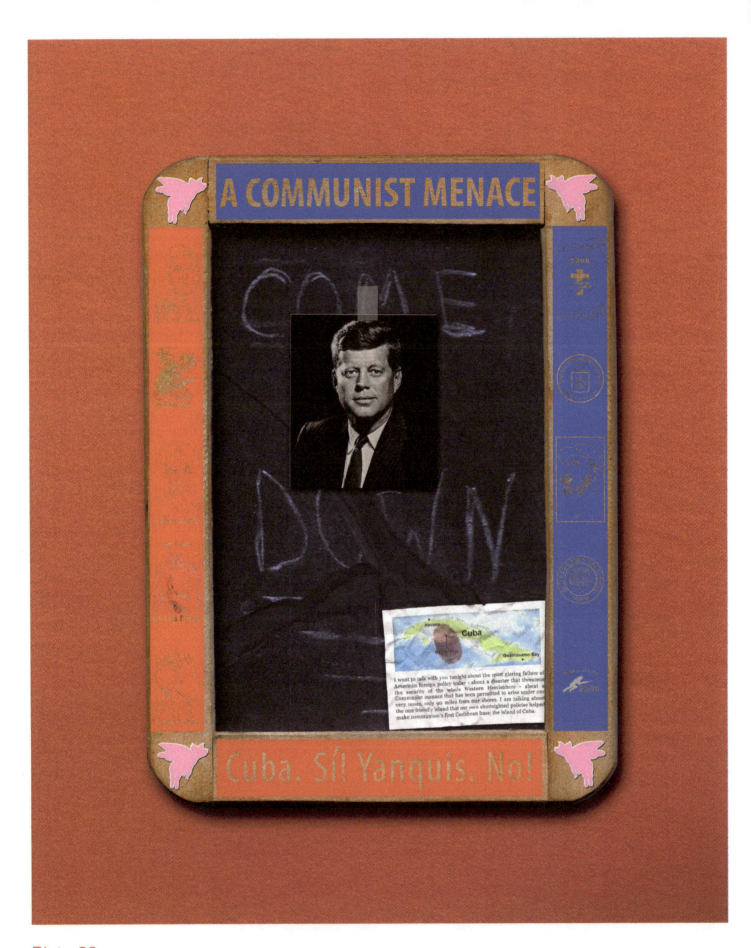

Plate 26
John A. O'Connor, *Revolution Illusion,* 2017-18. Digital Image, 21 x 17 in.

WHITE LIES MATTER

Kennedy had made a mess in Cuba at the Bay of Pigs. He had to do something to look good. The Apollo program of going to the Moon was quite a goal.
—Wally Schirra (Mercury, Gemini, and Apollo Astronaut)

How many Americans reminisce with nostalgia on the short-lived administration of John F. Kennedy? Do they see the Camelot that never was? Will we ever know what JFK might have accomplished—or in the case of Vietnam—might have avoided? The record he left is a hodgepodge. We may think of his strength and resolve during the Cuban Missile Crisis, when he stared down the Soviet Union and Khrushchev blinked. But earlier in his term, the Bay of Pigs disaster almost ended his presidency as it was barely beginning.

Although President Dwight David Eisenhower had ordered the CIA to instigate a strategy to invade Cuba and eliminate the regime of Fidel Castro, Kennedy, supposedly, did not learn of the plan to invade until after his election in 1960. (They didn't brief the president-elect back then?) After learning of the Eisenhower-CIA plan, Kennedy, with the advice and consent of his key administration officials, ordered the invasion of Cuba.[1] But, Kennedy brazenly declared, "I have previously stated, and I repeat now, that the United States plans no military intervention in Cuba."[2] (Ironically, as with almost everything the U.S. government reports about both covert and overt strategies and actions, the actual briefing of Kennedy appears to be in doubt. A thoroughly credible source clearly states that Kennedy was briefed on November 18, 1960—significantly prior to his inauguration—by CIA Director Allen Dulles and Richard Bissell the CIA's Deputy Director of Plans.[3])

Looking back at the day of April 15, 1961, we can now clearly see it as the beginning of a futile attack that the U.S. military would undoubtedly like to delete from American history books. The U.S. had been training anti-Castro troops in Guatemala and had bombers based in Nicaragua. The plan was designed (if you can call it that) to be two air strikes, followed by a nighttime invasion. Then, theoretically, the entire Cuban populace would rise up and join forces with Brigade 2506, defeat the Cuban armed forces, and Kennedy would celebrate the removal of a Communist dictator.

In preparing for the onslaught, the CIA painted World War II B-26B bombers to resemble Cuban airplanes—but they were apparently unaware that the Cuban planes they were supposed to imitate were B-26Cs that had a completely different nose from the B-26B.[4] However, even if that had been a successful deception, it would have made little difference in the outcome. The painted, American, [fake Cuban] B-26 bombers missed most of their targets anyway! Subsequent photos of the planes revealed that they were obviously American, not Cuban aircraft. Exposed, JFK cancelled the projected second air strike.[5]

However, the counter-revolutionary Cuban nationals known as Brigade 2506, backed by the CIA, did invade Cuba. The operation was a complete fiasco as Brigade 2506 was defeated by Castro's forces in just two days. The Bay of Pigs served only to strengthen Castro, weaken Kennedy, and embolden the Soviets to build bases in Cuba, leading to the Missile Crisis a year later.

I want to talk with you tonight about the most glaring failure of American foreign policy today - about a disaster that threatens the security of the whole Western Hemisphere - about a Communist menace that has been permitted to arise under our very noses, only 90 miles from our shores. I am talking about the one friendly island that our own shortsighted policies helped make communism's first Caribbean base: the island of Cuba.

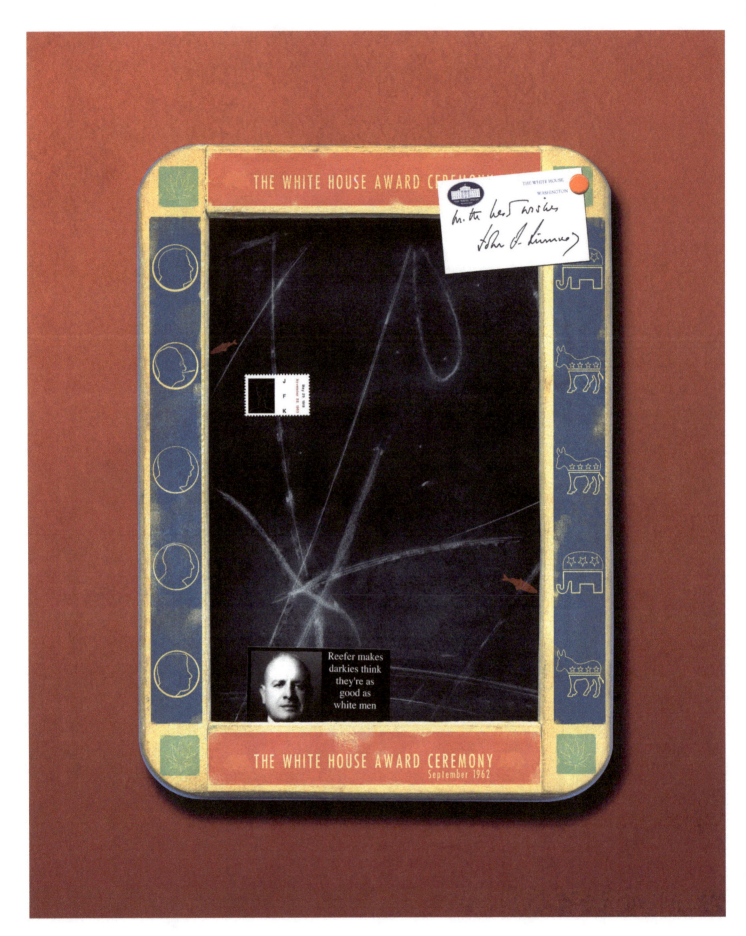

Plate 27

John A. O'Connor, *Profiles Encouraged,* 2016-17. Digital Image, 21 x 17 in.

WHITE LIES MATTER

PUBLIC PERCEPTION: Caring, intellectual, liberal leader.
PRIVATE REALITY: Indifference to fidelity, compassion, or morality.

September 27, 1962

It is my great pleasure to honor you [Harry J. Anslinger] for your outstanding record. You are a most distinguished servant and defender of the American people who are most indebted to you for you have symbolized the best in the service of our country with your unparalleled skill and knowledge, and you deserve our absolute respect, gratitude and admiration.

Signed,

John F. Kennedy[1]

WHO WAS THIS HARRY JACOB ANSLINGER?

Anslinger was a U.S. government official who served as the first commissioner of the Treasury Department's Federal Bureau of Narcotics (FBN), a staunch supporter of prohibition and the criminalization of drugs. He was **the man** who played the pivotal role in cannabis prohibition.

Anslinger worked for Republicans and Democrats from Herbert Hoover to John F. Kennedy. More than anyone in American history, he was responsible for the criminalization of marijuana. "Reefer makes darkies think they're as good

as white men" is perhaps his best known quote, but there are others despising jazz, "degenerate races" and white women who sought "sexual relations with Negroes."[2]

He ushered a bill through Congress and signed by President Franklin Roosevelt that designated marijuana as dangerous as heroin and cocaine. Almost immediately, cannabis began to account for more law enforcement activity than any other, and research on it virtually ceased because FBN wouldn't license its use by researchers outside of government.

JFK was a well-known fancier of women and cigars. But what of marijuana? Many stories exist about his use of cannabis—particularly with his legendary hordes of women. There are also numerous references to his use of pot for his well-known chronic back pain.[3]

"JFK used marijuana to deal with severe back pain, according to a few written accounts, including 'John F. Kennedy: A Biography,' which described this White House scene: "On the evening of July 16, 1962, according to [*Washington Post* executive] Jim Truitt, Kennedy and Mary Meyer smoked marijuana together. . . . The president smoked three of the six joints Mary brought to him. At first he felt no effects. Then he closed his eyes and refused a fourth joint. 'Suppose the Russians did something now,' he said."[4]

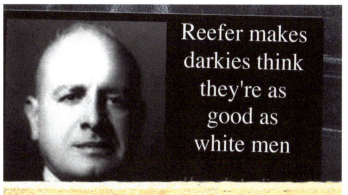

Reefer makes darkies think they're as good as white men

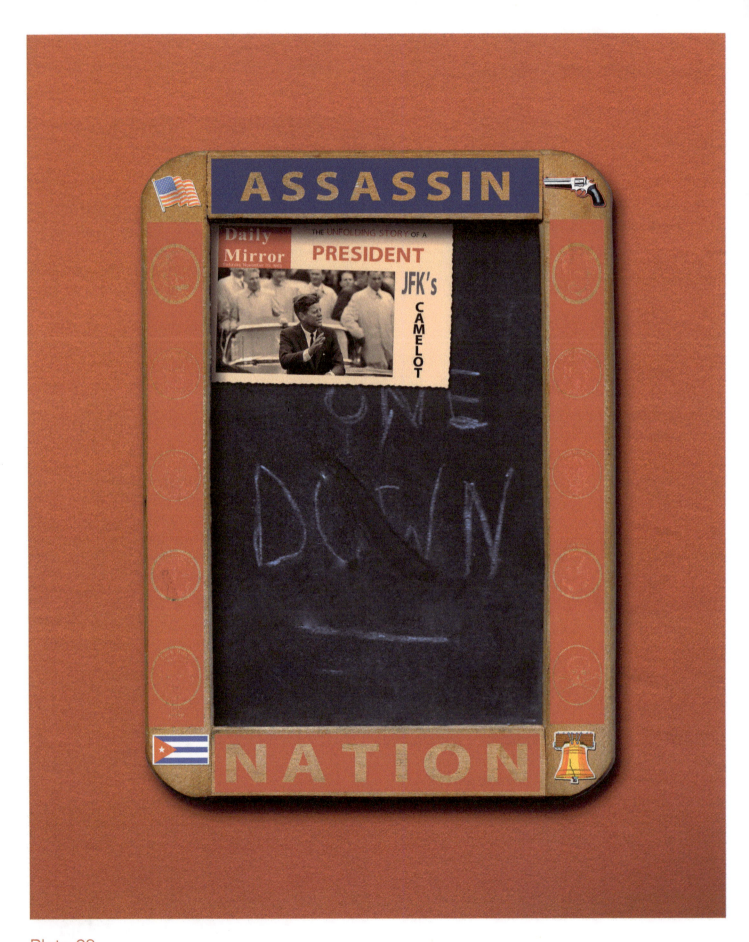

Plate 28

John A. O'Connor, *Assassin Nation,* 2017-18. Digital Image, 21 x 17 in.

WHITE LIES MATTER

Murder, it seems, is always in the news in the United States of America. The media (at least most of it) would have us believe that—excluding nations at war—we have the highest homicide rate in the world. However, according to Public Radio International, the U.S. is not even in the top 100—ranking 107th of 218 countries![1]

One reason so many Americans today (November 2017) are horrified by mass murders is that so many extensive shooting episodes have occurred during the past few years. But this is nothing new. While ordinary citizens attending an outdoor concert, going to school or church or a nightclub may get gunned down, murder by gunfire is not limited to merely ordinary folks.

Four American presidents were killed by gunfire while they were in office. They include Abraham Lincoln who was shot on April 14, 1865 by John Wilkes Booth—while attending a performance with his wife (and others) of Laura Keene's "Our American Cousin" at Ford's Theatre in our nation's capital. After holding office for only four months, James A. Garfield was shot by his attorney! William McKinley was gunned down on September 6, 1901. That prompted the U.S. Secret Service to, subsequently, take responsibility for protecting the president.[2] And, finally, John F. Kennedy was shot on November 22, 1963 in a motorcade in Dallas. This murder remains one of the most controversial events in American history.

Assassination attempts—all with guns—have been made on other U. S. Presidents including Andrew Jackson, Theodore Roosevelt, Franklin D. Roosevelt, Harry S. Truman, Richard Milhous Nixon, Gerald Ford (twice in the same month!), Jimmy Carter, Ronald Reagan, George

H. W. Bush (shortly after his term in office), Bill Clinton, George W. Bush, and Barack Obama.[3]

Ironically, JFK had a problem with Cuba, and especially with Fidel Castro. Most Americans probably never knew that Castro survived at least 638 attempts to murder him—mostly by the U.S. Central Intelligence Agency that even plotted with the mafia and enlisted two men on the FBI's most wanted list.[4]

Fifty-four years have passed since the assassination of JFK, yet the Trump administration still has not yet released all of the files related to that event and probably never will. Many of the files that will be released have already been redacted and are of little use. Therefore, these files containing additional details of JFK's assassination will continue to be tinder for conspiracy theories about his death. And, to add even more irony to the fire, over half of Americans believe that more than one person—Lee Harvey Oswald—was involved in the murder. Some believe that it was mafia-related, and others say it was the CIA. During the 2016 presidential campaign, Donald Trump even asserted that the father of Texas Republican Senator Ted Cruz might have been involved in the assassination plot.

But, this picture wouldn't be complete if it didn't, again, point the finger back at Cuba! [5]

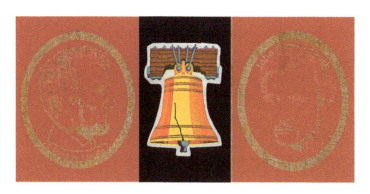

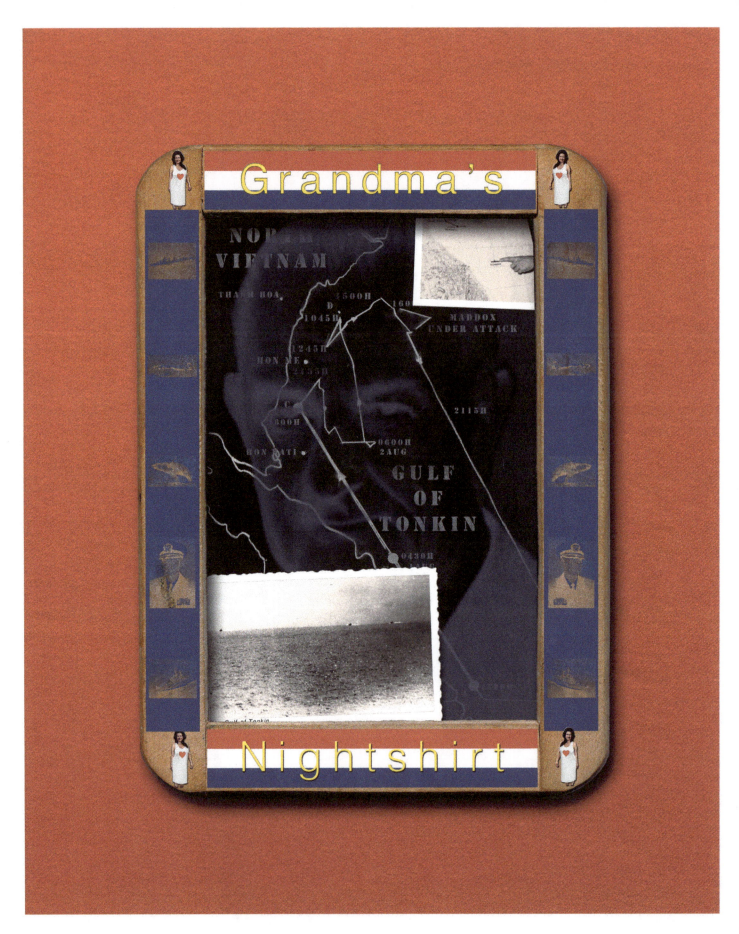

Plate 29

John A. O'Connor, *Grandma's Nightshirt,* 2017. Digital Image, 21 x 17 in.

WHITE LIES MATTER

"As Johnson later admitted, the [Gulf of Tonkin Resolution] was like Grandma's nightshirt–it covered everything."[1]

Many historians, and a few Americans who re-member it, think that the Vietnam War was a colossal mistake—maybe the greatest military miscalculation in U.S. history. That view probably changed when George W. Bush became president and invaded Iraq. It probably changed again now that the War in Afghanistan is the longest in American history.[2]

Numbers can sum up the enormity of the Vietnam War, but certainly not its devastation and resultant misery. More than 500,000 American soldiers fought there. Almost 60,000 died and 300,000 were wounded. The South Vietnamese had 850,000 troops and suffered from 170,000 to 220,000 casualties. In addition, South Vietnamese civilian fatalities were 200,000-400,000. In North Vietnam, over 50,000 civilians were killed, and its military suffered 400,000-1,000,000 deaths. **Yes that is one million deaths!** Additionally, more than 500,000 military were wounded.[3]

While the beginning of this war can be traced to an earlier time, major American participation in it was primarily the result of events that occurred in August 1964. "On August 2, two North Vietnamese torpedo boats in broad daylight engaged [*sic.*] USS Maddox, which was gathering communications intelligence in the Gulf of Tonkin. Two nights later, Maddox and the destroyer USS Turner Joy were on patrol in the Gulf and report-ed they were under attack. The pilot of an F-8E Crusader did not see any ships in the area where the enemy was reported, and years later crew members said they never saw attacking craft. An electrical storm was interfering with the ships' radar and may have given the impression of ap-proaching attack boats."[4]

There was significant "confusion" in Washington, D.C. about what was really going on. "In Hawaii, Pacific Fleet Commander-in-Chief Admiral U.S. Grant Sharp was receiving Captain Herrick's reports by flash message traffic, not voice reports. At 0248 in the Gulf, Herrick sent another report in which he changed his previous story:
"Certain that original ambush was bonafide. Details of action following present a confusing picture. Have interviewed witnesses who made positive visual sightings of cockpit lights or similar passing near MADDOX. Several reported torpedoes were probably boats themselves which were observed to make several close passes on MADDOX. Own ship screw noises on rudders may have accounted for some. At present cannot even estimate number of boats involved. TURNER JOY reports two torpedoes passed near her."[5] U.S. Secretary of Defense Robert McNamara, the Joint Chiefs of Staff, the National Military Command, and the Pacific Command all exchanged calls. McNamara even asked, "Was there a possibility that there had been no attack?"[6]

"Other intelligence supported the belief that an attack had occurred." In response, President Johnson ordered air strikes against North Vietnam that included bombing an oil depot and its naval bases.[7] Johnson then, in a televised address to the American people about the purported attacks on U.S. ships, requested a congressional resolution empowering him to conduct war in Southeast Asia.

On August 7, 1964, the United States Congress passed the Gulf of Tonkin Resolution that authorized "the president, as commander-in-chief, to take all necessary measures to repel any armed attack against the forces of the US and to prevent further aggression."[8] Transferring war powers from Congress to the president was—many believe—LBJ's legacy achievement—probably because it has been used over and over again by subsequent presidents to wage war without authorization by Congress. Ironically, one "year after the incident, Johnson said to then Press Secretary Bill Moyers, 'For all I know, our Navy was shooting at whales out there.' "[9]

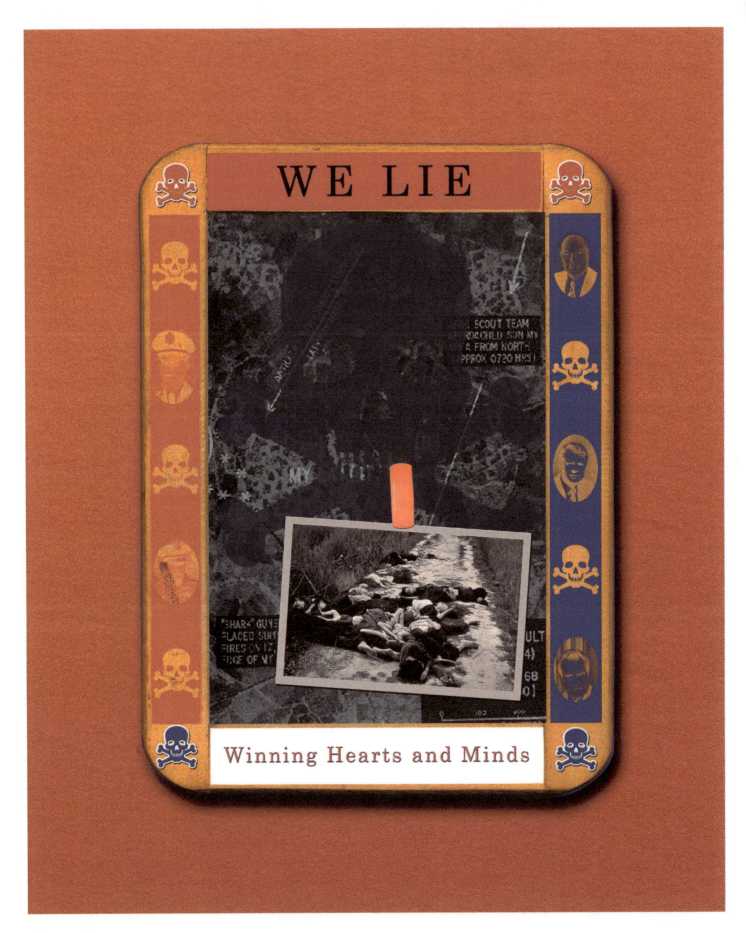

Plate 30
John A. O'Connor, *Winning Hearts and Minds,* 2017. Digital Image, 21 x 17 in.

WHITE LIES MATTER

The Mỹ Lai Massacre was also known as the "Pinkville Massacre." It featured "Band-Aids," "Birds," " Fugazi," possibly "Long Pigs," "Nuts to Butts," and—in all likelihood—a lot of other colloquialisms that contributed to a major "Soup Sandwich."[1]

A large number of unarmed Vietnamese were murdered on March 16, 1968. The U.S. army reported the number of enemy dead at 128. There was only one American casualty—a U.S. soldier who was shot in the foot. (He did it to himself!). So, what did the U.S. military decide to do about this incident? It just covered it up—temporarily.

Almost two years later, mass graves containing more than 500 bodies were found. And, in March 1971, 2nd Lieutenant, William L. "Rusty" Calley was found guilty of murder by a military court at Ft. Benning, Georgia. He was sentenced to life in prison after the longest court-martial in U.S. history.[2]

Gang-raped and mutilated women made up part of this glorious American escapade by Charlie Company. Apparently at least thirty U.S. army personnel were aware of this event, but only fourteen were ever accused of crimes. But all charges were dismissed except those against William Calley.[3]

How did this happen? Charlie Company had at least 100 soldiers involved. Commanding officer, Captain Ernest Medina, ordered the action (massacre?) apparently convinced that the area was a Vietcong stronghold. After all, the Vietnamese were Vietcong. Who could tell the difference? They were all "gooks." Sound familiar?[4]

Who was given the assignment to investigate what had happened? It was Army major Colin Powell. "Colin Powell's report seemed to refute the allegations of wrongdoing and stated, 'Relations between American soldiers and the Vietnamese people are excellent.' "[5] Then-Georgia Governor Jimmy Carter described Calley as a "scapegoat" and proclaimed American Fighting Men's Day. The next month, Carter "denied that he had ever supported Lieutenant Calley or condoned his actions."[6] Calley was released after serving only three years of his life sentence that had been repeatedly reduced by appeals and the Secretary of the Army before he was paroled by Richard Nixon in 1974.[7]

(I have read and re-read these conflicting numbers (see above) many times, and I think that the "conflicting text" actually supports the lies, confusion, and deception of the reporting at that time. I don't se how I/we could ever get to the truth of this issue. Left as it is written, it probably will cause confusion. Removed—or further "explained"—it will still confuse readers.)

Why were we in Vietnam anyway? John F. Kennedy was determined to show strength against communism—especially after his Bay of Pigs, Cuba debacle.[8] Lyndon Johnson said, "we must be ready to fight in Viet-Nam, but the ultimate victory will depend upon the hearts and the minds of the people who actually live out there."[9] There is a much earlier version of the phrase "hearts and minds": "And the peace of God, which transcends all understanding, will guard your hearts and your minds in Christ Jesus."[10] Since wars are frequently called crusades, could Kennedy and Johnson have been thinking about this verse in the Bible?

And, finally, did anything good come out of the Mỹ Lai Massacre? After Calley was sentenced, American sentiment against the war in Vietnam began to change. Ironically, although a large majority of Americans opposed the Calley verdict, just two weeks later polls, for the first time, showed that a majority of Americans now opposed the war in Vietnam.[11]

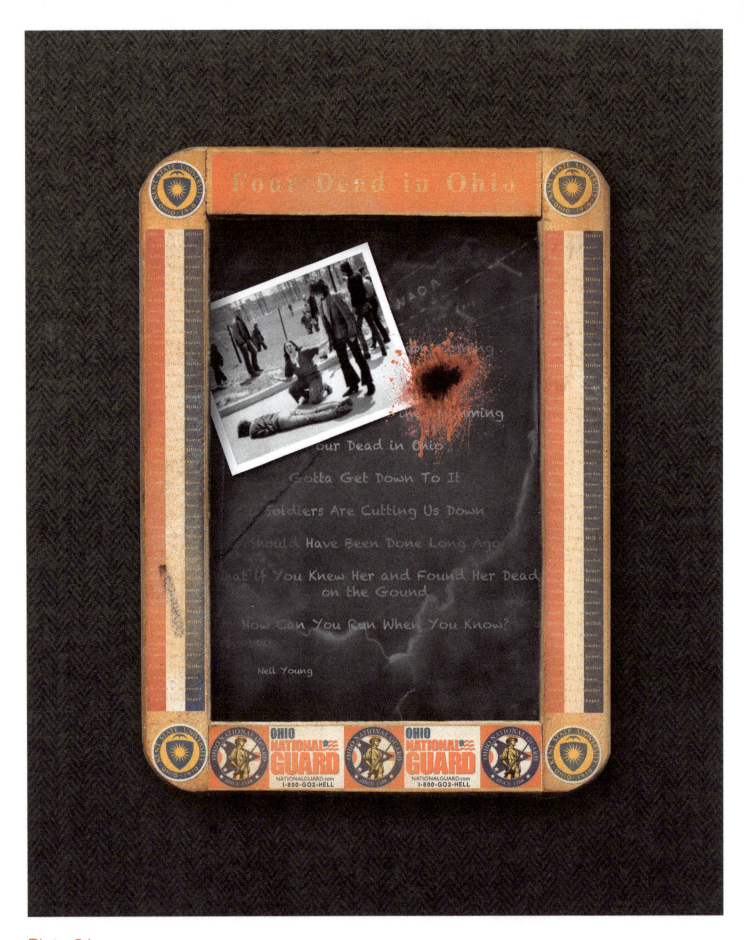

Plate 31

John A. O'Connor, *Four Dead in Ohio,* 2017. Digital Image, 21 x 17 in.

WHITE LIES MATTER

our Dead

"Pigs off Campus!"
"Pigs off Campus!"
"Pigs off Campus!"
"Pigs off Campus!"

At the end of April 1970, the U.S. decided to expand the war in Vietnam by invading neighboring Cambodia. President Nixon said that an additional 150,000 soldiers were needed to support this invasion, and that they would need to be drafted.

Student protests erupted throughout the United States, but two were deadly. The first one, and by far the most famous, took place at Kent State University in Ohio. When students set fire to the ROTC building on campus, Ohio Governor James A. Rhodes deployed nearly 1,000 Ohio National Guardsmen to the campus. On May 4, 1970, it was reported that 28 guardsmen fired on a crowd of students, killing four and wounding nine more. The campus was shut down, and protests spread nationwide. As many as 500 other college and university campuses became the center of massive protests against the war in Vietnam (and Cambodia).

The United States so-called Justice Department at first refused to investigate. However, a subsequent Commission on Campus Unrest decided that the guardsmen's killing and wounding of the Kent students was "unnecessary, unwarranted, and inexcusable." Sometime later, a grand jury did indict eight guardsmen but dismissed charges because of lack of evidence.

However, what was not widely reported at that time (it was basically ignored) was that two black students were murdered by police and Mis-

sissippi State Highway Patrolmen and nine more were wounded. Was this incident just overlooked, or was it deemed unimportant by the media because it occurred at Jackson State University–an all black school?[1]

And, was this the entire story? Not at all! According to *The New York Times,* in an article from May 5, 1970 written by John Kifner titled "8 Hurt as Shooting Follows Reported Sniping at Rally," the guardsmen only fired on the students after the guardsmen were fired on by a sniper and the guardsmen were being threatened by students who began to surround them. Kifner, who says he was at the scene, said there was no sniper fire. None! Several rocks had been thrown, however.[2]

Ironically, on May 3, 1970, Ohio governor Rhodes said, "We're asking the legislature that any person throwing a rock, brick or stone at a law enforcement agent of Ohio, a sheriff, policeman, highway patrol, national guard becomes a felony. . . ."[3]

So, it was just a student protest of a far away war. Not according to Ohio Governor Rhodes who said of the protesting Kent State students, "They're the worst type of people that we harbor in America. I think that we're up against the strongest, well-trained, militant, revolutionary group that has ever assembled in America.[4]

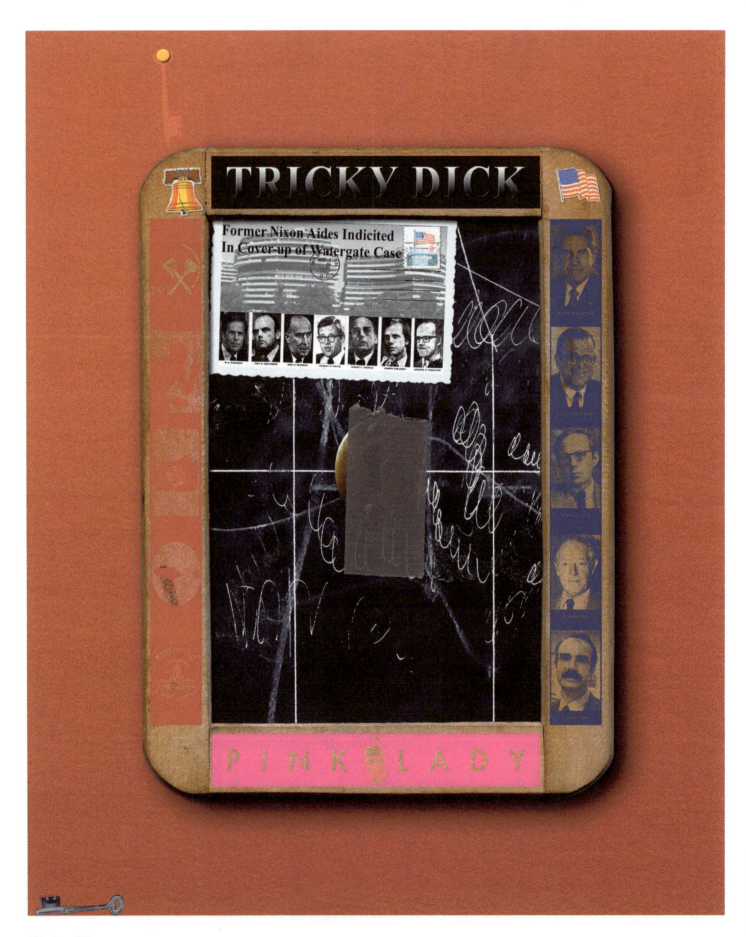

Plate 32

John A. O'Connor, *Tricky Dick,* 2018. Digital Image, 21 x 17 in.

TRICKY DICK

On June 17, 1972, just months before Richard Milhous Nixon's reelection to a second term, five burglars broke into the headquarters of the Democratic National Committee located in the Watergate—a Washington, D.C. hotel and office complex. Fortunately, security spotted them, informed the metro police, and they were arrested. Caught with surveillance and electronic equipment, they awaited arraignment in a federal court while the FBI initiated an investigation.[1]

Nixon denied any knowledge of, or connection to the burglary. But, at the same time, two *Washington Post* reporters, Bob Woodward and Carl Bernstein, investigating the incident, concluded that there were connections between the thieves and Nixon's reelection campaign. In the meantime Nixon was reelected that November in one of the greatest landslides in American history.[2]

Just ten days after President Nixon's second inauguration, the trial of the Watergate conspirators expanded to the burglars and two accomplices—resulting in five guilty pleas (by former CIA member E. Howard Hunt and four others) and two convictions for conspiracy, burglary, and bugging the Democratic National Committee Headquarters at the Watergate. These latter two were former FBI agent G. Gordon Liddy, and another former CIA employee James McCord. McCord, appropriately, was the security director of the Committee to Re-elect the President—acroynym: CREEP! In the days and months ahead, John Dean, the White House Counsel, H. R. Haldeman, Nixon's Chief of Staff, John D. Ehrlichman, Assistant for Domestic Affairs, and Attorney General Richard Kleindienst all resigned.

In May 1973, Archibald Cox was appointed Special Prosecutor for the Watergate probe. He and the Senate Select Committee on Presidential Campaign Activities (chaired by Senator Sam Ervin, D, NC) subsequently ran head-on into Nixon's increasingly obstinate nature. Both made requests for White House tapes and Nixon refused.

This Soap Opera became known as the "Saturday Night Massacre." As the spectacle escalated over the summer and into the fall, Nixon ordered the firing of Archibald Cox, but instead of that happening, Nixon's own Attorney General Elliot Richardson and Deputy Attorney General William Ruckelhaus resigned.[3] Cox subsequently got fired anyway by Solicitor General Robert Bork (an eventual Supreme Court nominee). Then, Leon Jaworski was named Special Prosecutor.

On November 17, in Orlando, Florida, in response to increasing suspicions, and in front of 400 Associated Press editors, Nixon (in)famously proclaimed, "I am not a crook." While he was, ostensibly, talking about not profiting from public service, that quote defined his entire political career.[4] By July 1974, the House Judiciary Committee had approved three articles of impeachment against Nixon and sent it to the full House for a vote. On August 8, Nixon told a nationwide TV audience that he would resign, and the next day he did. A month later, he received a full pardon from then-President Ford. But it didn't end there. In January 1975, Nixon's former Attorney General John N. Mitchell and his former aide Erlichmann and his Chief of Staff Haldeman were convicted of obstruction of justice. Two years later, Nixon defended himself by uttering, "I'm saying that when the president does it, it means it's not illegal." Deep Throat turned out to be the former Associate Director of the FBI, Mark Felt, who believed that he "was doing the right thing." He was convicted in 1980 for conspiracy for authorizing agents to break into homes without search warrants.

By the way, Nixon didn't get the name "Tricky Dick" because of the Watergate Scandal. He already had earned that moniker from Helen Gahagan Douglas in the 1950 California Senate race whom he had branded as the "pink lady." Her response was that Nixon was "Tricky Dick."[5]

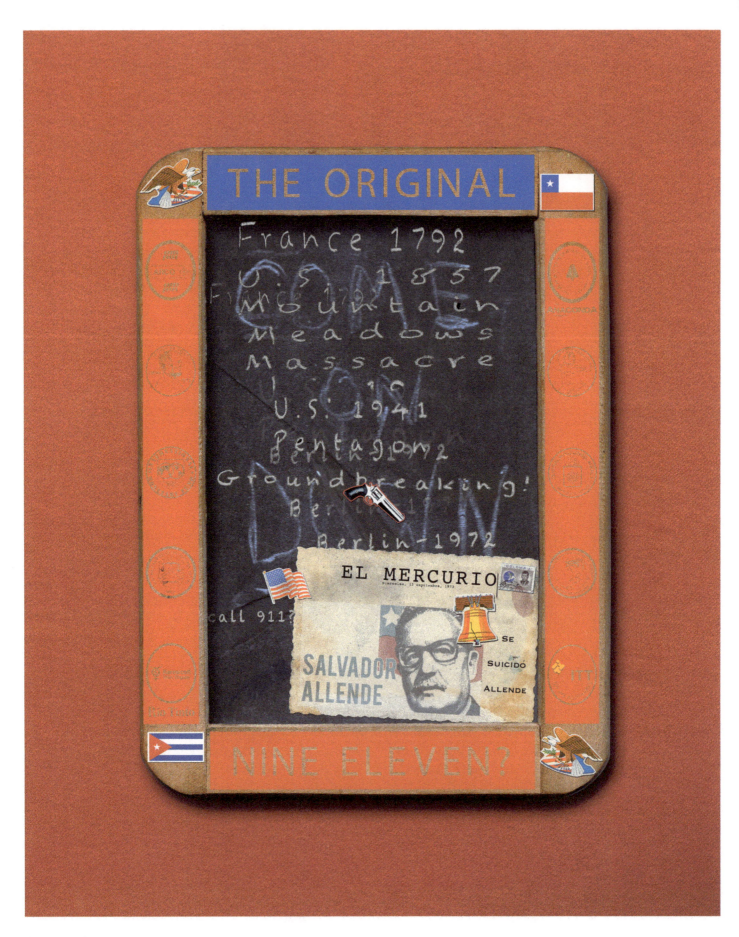

Plate 33

John A. O'Connor, *Co-incidents,* 2018. Digital Image, 21 x 17 in.

WHITE LIES MATTER

Most Americans probably don't know that the United States has repeatedly interfered with the Chilean government. Before the War of 1812 (the U.S. versus Britain—another war about "trade issues"), the U.S. already had a special envoy in Chile. By 1891, following the War of the Pacific, the U.S. was again meddling in Chile's internal affairs—this time in the Chilean Civil War. By the end of World War I, the U.S. had replaced Great Britain as the major source of economic control in Chile. United States mining giant Anaconda Copper Mining Company (a subsidiary of ARCO which is now a subsidiary of BP) made most of its money from its Chilean copper operation—then the largest mine in the world. Kennecott Utah Copper LLC (a subsidiary of Rio Tinto Group) is also one of the world's largest mining corporations. As late as 1970, these two companies controlled as much as 20% of Chile's GDP.[1]

A number of sources suggest that economic control exerted by U.S. corporations in Chile and American government support of Chilean politicians sympathetic with U.S. interests, eventually led to the election of Salvador Allende as president of Chile in 1970.

Less well known is that U.S. plans to stop Allende began in the 1950s. Again, the tactics used by the Americans were focused on trade. As the Chilean government reduced tariffs, its economy was overwhelmed by American imports. These policies were supported by American banks, the U.S. Treasury Department, and even the International Monetary Fund. Consequently, many Chilean workers became more and more angry, and many began to consider Allende's socialist policies as a solution to their problems.

But American opposition to Allende was also based on his denunciation of JFK's failed Bay of Pigs Invasion of Cuba, and Kennedy's fear that Chile was about to become another Cuba. During the 1964 Chilean presidential election, the U.S. Central Intelligence Agency provided at least $3 million to support Allende's opposition. Not only did the CIA influence the election, it was also involved in "human rights abuses or in covering up any human rights abuses in Chile. . . ."[2]

Of course, by the time Salvador Allende was finally elected president of Chile in 1970, Kennedy was long gone, but his clandestine activities had been fully embraced by then-U.S. President Richard Nixon. According to reports, in 1973 Nixon ordered the CIA "to attempt to foment a coup."[3]

It is ironic that the United States was so paranoid about Allende's election. Chile, according to many sources, had a long tradition of democracy—somewhat unusual in Latin America. Yes, Allende was a founder of the Socialist Party in Chile, but he supported a peaceful, democratic transition to socialism—a rather unusual position since most "socialist" countries were created by revolutions.

In 1973 the Chilean government was taken over in a military coup on September 11. This dictatorship, led by General Augusto Pinochet, ruled Chile from 1973 to1990. It focused primarily on economic "reforms" based on policies obtained in large part from the Department of Economics at the University of Chicago and reinforced by University of Chicago-trained economists at the Universidad Católica de Chile. While some economic reforms were accomplished during this period, state-sponsored terrorism and torture also occurred.[4]

On that same day, September 11, 1973, President Salvador Allende's life ended. Reports claim it was suicide, but doubts remain to this day what role the U.S. CIA may have played.[5]

Plate 34
John A. O'Connor, *Just Plain Jimmy,* 2016-17. Digital Image, 21 x 17 in.

WHITE LIES MATTER

If I get back in, I'm going to [expletive] the Jews.[1]

—President James Earl Carter, Jr.

James Earl Carter, Jr., known to all as "Jimmy" was the 39th President of the United States (1977-1981). Carter's presidency is probably best remembered for the Iran Hostage Crisis of 1979, but it was back in the news as recently as May 2, 2017 when, "For inexplicable reasons, the Trump administration apparently pressured Argentina to back out of its announced plan to give President Jimmy Carter the nation's highest honor."[2]

Jimmy Carter was a graduate of the Naval Academy, a naval officer, and, following his presidency, a noted humanitarian active in Habitat for Humanity, a winner of the Nobel Peace Prize in 2002, and a peanut farmer. But, as President, he is known for creating the Department of Education and the Department of Energy. One of his major priorities was to reduce U.S. dependence on foreign oil. along with energy consumption. He also fostered the Camp David Peace Accords–a peace treaty between Israel and Egypt.

Critics faulted him for many things—especially the energy crisis of 1979, not stopping the Soviet invasion of Afghanistan, the U.S. boycott of the Summer Olympics of 1980 held in Moscow, his brother, Billy, for a plethora of reasons, and Bert Lance, Jimmy's Director of the Office of Management and Budget.

Carter was a complicated person. Like an onion with many layers, if you peeled them off one by one, you would find a Christian, a Born Again Christian, a strong supporter of civil rights, a friend of many black people, a supporter of infamous segregationist George Wallace, a critic of Martin Luther King, a supporter of segregationist Lester Maddox, a supporter of the death penalty—then not a supporter of the death penalty, and a person quite ambivalent about the Mỹ Lai Massacre in Vietnam while at the same time, as Governor of Georgia, he created "American Fighting Man's Day."

Significant irony also exists with Carter's run for president in 1976. Virtually unknown outside of Georgia, he had a national name recognition of just two percent! Yet with the Watergate Scandal still haunting the Republicans and Gerald Ford considered a weak and bumbling candidate, Carter ran as a populist outsider untainted by corrupt Washington, D.C. Although he did not promise to "drain the swamp," he did seek support from conservative Christian voters and people in rural areas who felt overlooked. The year 1976 looks, in retrospect, eerily similar to 2016.[3]

Jimmy Carter is credited with many noble concerns and actions following his presidency such as asking that the infamous American base at Guantánamo Bay be closed, amazingly expressing his concern that the "Religious Right" had excessive power in U.S. politics, and asking for a worldwide end to the war on drugs. But he also supported then-Venezuelan President Chávez, regularly criticized Israel, and worked with North Korean leaders to, supposedly, end their nuclear ambitions. He also invoked Jesus Christ's opposition to abortion—hence Carter's own problems upholding Roe v. Wade. Yet in 2000 he broke with the Southern Baptist Convention over its position on women's rights.[4]

Just Plain Jimmy really wasn't very plain after all.

Plate 35

John A. O'Connor, *In Sight,* 2016-17. Digital Image, 21 x 17 in.

WHITE LIES MATTER

"A few months ago I told the American people I did not trade arms for hostages. My heart and my best intentions still tell me that's true, but the facts and the evidence tell me it is not."[1]

This slate is about a very complicated period of time during Ronald Reagan's presidency, and it reveals something that most Americans think is a relatively new development: "alternate facts," or "fake news."

It contains a number of images that relate specifically to what became known as the Iran-Contra Affair. That incident was an extremely murky period in U.S. history primarily because, like all political scandals, a significant amount of information was hidden, obscured, destroyed, or merely lied about. What was subsequently reported as happening was that Lieutenant Colonel Oliver North of the U.S. National Security Council (NSC), (mug shot card of him tucked under the frame in the top right corner of the slate) secretly arranged to have some of the proceeds of U.S. weapon sales to Iran diverted to fund the anti-Sandinista forces (hence the term Contras) in Nicaragua. The weapons were supposed to be shipped to Israel first, and then delivered by

Israel to Iran. Ultimately, this event was an arms-for-hostages deal that President Reagan finally admitted on March 4, 1987.

A number of administration officials were indicted, eleven convicted (some of which were vacated), and the rest eventually pardoned by President George H. W. Bush.

How ironic that this affair in the 1980s was subsequently classified as "post-truth politics." So, you see, fake news and alternate facts are really nothing new. And, just like today, the underlying aspects of a so-called "war on terrorism" were being played out with Iran as the terrorist agent but with the zany notion that the weapon sales would only go to supposedly moderate Iranians.[2] Do you really believe that? The weapons were for the Contras! Reagan said, "They are our brothers, these freedom fighters, and we owe them our help. I've spoken recently of the freedom fighters of Nicaragua. You know the truth about them. You know who they're fighting and why. They are the moral equal of our Founding Fathers and the brave men and women of the French Resistance. We cannot turn away from them, for the struggle here is not right versus left; it is right versus wrong."[3]

Some of the weapons that Iran received included at least 120 Hawk anti-aircraft missiles (Homing All the Way Killer) plus hundreds of spare parts and at least 2,400 TOW anti-tank missile launchers (Tube-launched, Optically-tracked, Wireless-guided).[4]

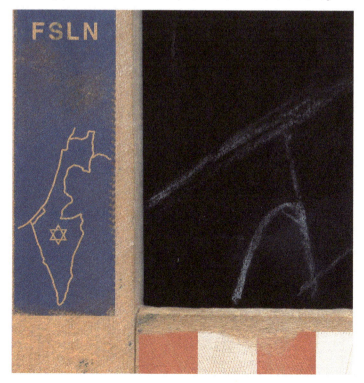

Plate 36
John A. O'Connor, *Saint Ronald,* 2016-17. Digital Image, 21 x 17 in.

WHITE LIES MATTER

Within the covers of the Bible are the answers for all the problems men face.[1]

WARS

"Ronald Reagan was a saint, a commanding leader, the gold standard of principled conservatism against whom all current and future Republicans should be measured."[2] Really?

Reagan was the most popular president since Franklin Delano Roosevelt, right? Well, no! During his two terms in office, Reagan—as popular as he appears in posterity—was less popular than Dwight D. Eisenhower, John F. Kennedy and even Lyndon B. Johnson. In addition, during his first two years, his approval ratings were even lower than those of Jimmy Carter![3]

Reagan was a devoutly and deeply religious evangelical Christian. Uh huh. Okay, then what was Ronald Reagan's position on religion? St. Ronnie overwhelmingly defeated President Jimmy Carter, a true evangelical Christian, in the presidential election of 1980, and he did so with the strong support of evangelical Christian voters. How could this happen? As we all know, evangelical Christians vehemently oppose abortion, and by 1980, Reagan did too. But, in 1967, as Governor of California, he signed the most liberal abortion law in the United States. Then, in 1986 the complete reversal came in his State of the Union speech to Congress. In it he said, "America will never be whole as long as the right to life granted by our Creator is denied to the unborn."[4]

Well, Ronald Reagan, like all good conservative Republicans, unequivocally supported the Second Amendment and the right to bear arms. Right? Then, why, in 1967, did he say, he didn't "know of any sportsman who leaves his home with a gun to go out into the field to hunt or for target shooting who carries that gun loaded."[5] Then he signed the Mulford Act of 1967 that banned carrying loaded weapons in public. By the way, it was strongly supported by the National Rifle Association and Mulford was a Republican.[6] My, how times have changed. Guess Bob Dylan was right after all!

How about worker's rights? After all, Reagan was a union man himself who became President of the Screen Actors Guild (SAG) in 1947 and led it in its first three strikes. In 1981, he said, "I hope you'll forgive me if I point with some pride to the fact that I'm the first president of the United States to hold a lifetime membership in an AFL-CIO union."[7] And, soon he will be inducted into the Hall of Honor of the United States Department of Labor. Isn't this honor somewhat odd since Reagan's relationship with labor during his presidency was highlighted by his firing of more than 11,000 striking union air traffic controllers? And, while he was Governor of California, he openly opposed the organization of immigrant farm workers who were led by Dolores Huerta and Cesar Chavez. Ironically, he will join both of them in the Department of Labor Hall of Honor.[8]

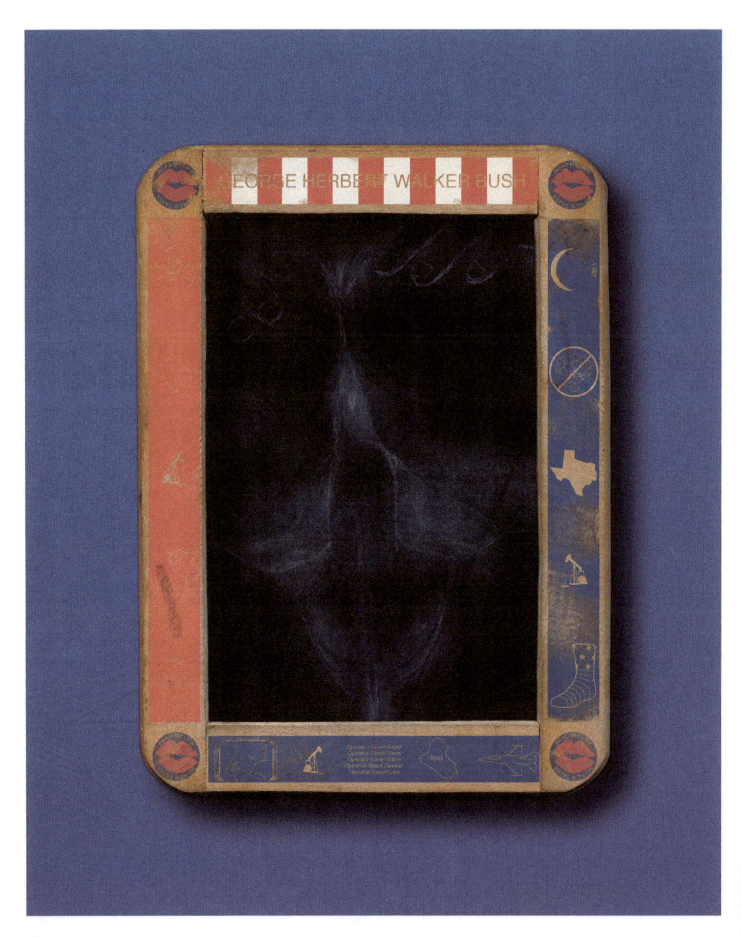

Plate 37
John A. O'Connor, *Magog Be With You,* 2016-17. Digital Image, 21 x 17 in.

WHITE LIES MATTER

"Read my lips: no new taxes."[1]

The first quote, uttered by presidential nominee George H. W. Bush at the 1988 Republican National Convention probably cost him the 1992 re-election campaign against Bill Clinton since he did just the opposite. Ironically, many people believe that it helped him win the 1988 election.

Known for his "thousand points of light,"[3] Bush actually established a foundation promoting volunteerism and service. But do you remember Panama and Operation Just Cause? Before the end of his first year as President of the United States, Magog launched Operation Just Cause—an invasion of Panama to capture Manuel Noriega (ironically a CIA asset) for drug trafficking. What was rarely mentioned in the accolades Bush received for one of the best, cleanest, quickest, most successful military actions in American history, was that the U.S. had bombed a poor Panamanian city called El Chorillo. Eyewitnesses labeled the killing of thousands of villagers and displacing tens of thousands "Guernica" or "little Hiroshima." It was another military action to preserve democracy. George Will labeled it, lovingly, "militant democracy," thus giving

an entirely new meaning to that "thousand points of light" especially when you see bombs going off every two minutes for twelve hours.[4]

But, who or what is Magog? The literature on this supposedly biblical character is highly disputed. However, it is the name assigned to the incoming member of Yale University's most famous (or infamous) secret society—the Skull and Bones—the new Bonesman who has had the most sexual experience![5] Really! George H. W. Bush!

Speaking of bombs going off every two minutes, what about our "good war" in Iraq? Many Americans believe that our first war in Iraq, begun by George H. W. Bush, was a "just war," and the war started by his son, George W. Bush, was a "bad war." Why? "Domino Theory" time again.

I like a colorful sock. I'm a sock man.[2]

That bad old Saddam Hussein wasn't going to stop in Kuwait. He wanted to invade and conquer Saudi Arabia—our major oil supplier. At the time, Bush said, "I took this action to assist the Saudi Arabian government in the defense of its homeland."[6] He also said, "In the life of a nation, we're called upon to define who we are and what we believe. Sometimes these choices are not easy. But today as President, I ask for your support in a decision I've made to stand up for what's right and condemn what's wrong, all in the cause of peace."[7]

Operation Desert Shield
Operation Desert Storm
Operation Desert Sabre
Operation Desert Farewell
Operation Desert Calm

IRAQ

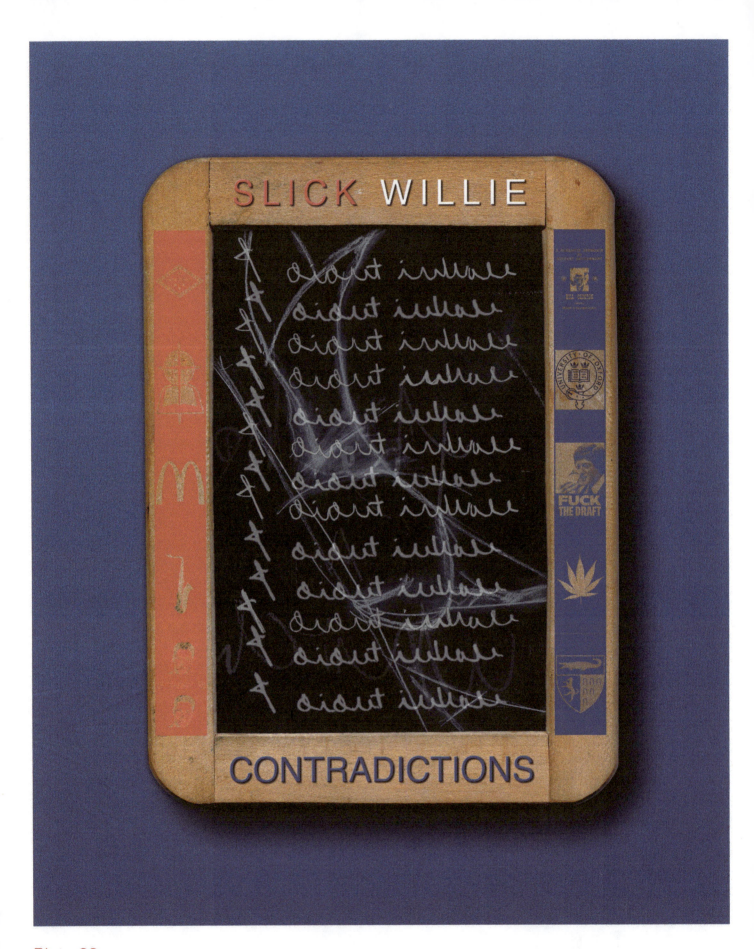

Plate 38
John A. O'Connor, *Slick Willie,* 2018. Digital Image, 21 x 17 in.

WHITE LIES MATTER

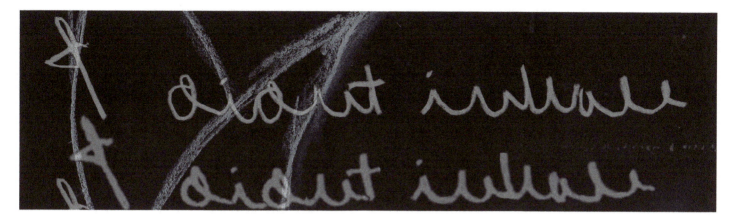

William Jefferson Blythe III[1]—who Americans know as Bill Clinton, the 42nd President of the United States, was twenty-two years old when he arrived in England as a Rhodes Scholar at the world famous University of Oxford. One of only thirty-two Americans who had received this prestigious award in 1968, Clinton decided to pursue a degree in politics—a program that he never finished perhaps because he had a number of other things on his mind.

During this time, his real focus was on the Vietnam War—a war that he, supposedly, vigorously opposed—arguably out of a sincere conviction, but also because he was extremely fearful that he would be drafted if he were back home in the United States.[2] This latter position is supported by his comments in a letter to "Mark" dated November 3, 1968, in which Clinton states, "I am getting in pretty good physical shape. Have lost my belly and a lot of flab playing basketball and rugby. These British rugby players are pretty tough. I have already suffered a cut over the left eye and, if I play much more, I'm liable to get hurt so bad I'll flunk my draft physical. Wishful thinking."[3]

Ironically, while at Oxford, Bill Clinton also appeared to espouse pro-feminist ideas before exposing his enduring sexist views while attending a lecture in 1970 by Germaine Greer—a well-known voice in the feminist movement. Clinton was the first to respond to the question and answer period. Commenting on Greer's remarks that working-class men were far better sexual partners than bourgeois ones, Bill, dressed "in a pink poplin suit and ginger beard," stood up and asked, "In case you ever decide to give bourgeois men another chance, can I give you my phone number?"[4]

It wasn't until March 1992 that Bill Clinton revealed that he had used marijuana while he was at Oxford. He said, "I've never broken a state law. But when I was in England I experimented with marijuana a time or two, and I didn't like it. I didn't inhale it, and never tried it again."[5] Johnny Carson, then host of "The Tonight Show," cracked, "That's the trouble with the Democrats. Even when they do something wrong, they don't do it right."[6]

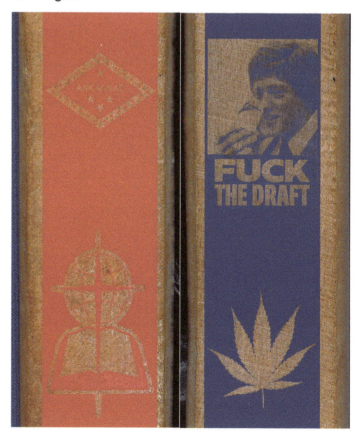

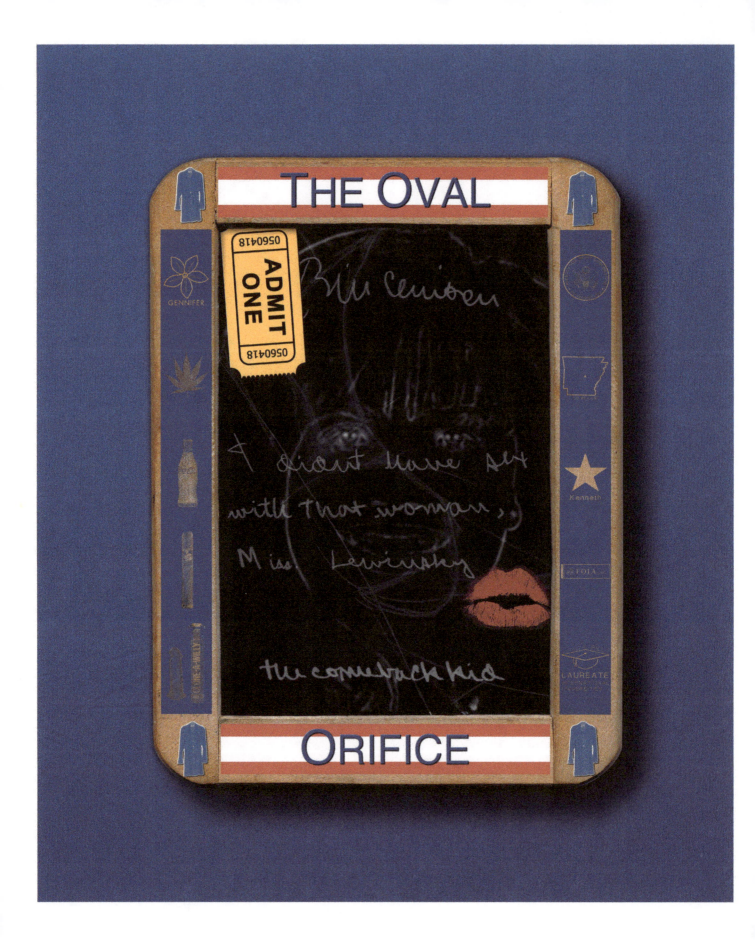

Plate 39

John A. O'Connor, *The Oval Orifice,* 2016-17. Digital Image, 21 x 17 in.

WHITE LIES MATTER

"I did not have sexual relations with that woman, Miss Lewinsky."[1]

The Monica Lewinsky Scandal was also known as Tailgate,[2] Sexgate, and Zippergate.[3] It was not the first public disclosure of President Clinton's sexual peccadillos, but it is the most infamous. Other women who have accused Bill Clinton of sexual misconduct include Juanita Broaddrick who accused him of raping her in 1978. Then there is Paula Jones who claims that he made improper sexual advances on her and also exposed himself. This incident occurred in 1991 and was finally resolved in 1998 when Clinton paid out $850,000 to settle. Then, there was Kathleen Willey who, as a White House volunteer in 1993, claimed Clinton grabbed and kissed her in the private study in the Oval Office. This incident was brought up again during Hillary Clinton's failed presidential run in 2016. These incidents are all referred to as "non-consensual encounters."[4]

Numerous other women have alleged that they had affairs with Bill Clinton. They include Gennifer Flowers who apparently had at least a twelve-year sexual relationship with Bill before he became president. He actually admitted that he had a sexual relationship with Flowers, but that it wasn't for twelve years.

A woman named Dolly Kyle Browning, a Clinton high school friend, claimed that she and Bill had sex from the mid-1970s until January 1992. And Elizabeth Ward Gracen, who was Miss America of 1982, said she had sex with Bill that year although he denies the allegation. There was also Miss Arkansas 1958, Sally Perdue, who claimed to have had an affair with Bill Clinton while he was governor of Arkansas.[5]

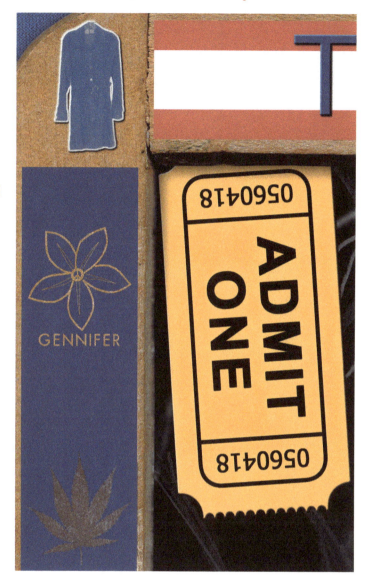

And then there was also Eileen Wellstone who accused Clinton of sexual assault in 1969 in England while Bill was a student at Oxford University.[6] Another allegation came from a legal secretary named Carolyn Moffet. She claims that in 1979, she fled Clinton's hotel room in Little Rock when he demanded certain sex acts. Bill Clinton was also accused of trying to seduce one Becky Brown—his daughter's (Chelsea Clinton) nanny.[7]

And, apparently there are even more!

I mean just look at this impeccable source!!!

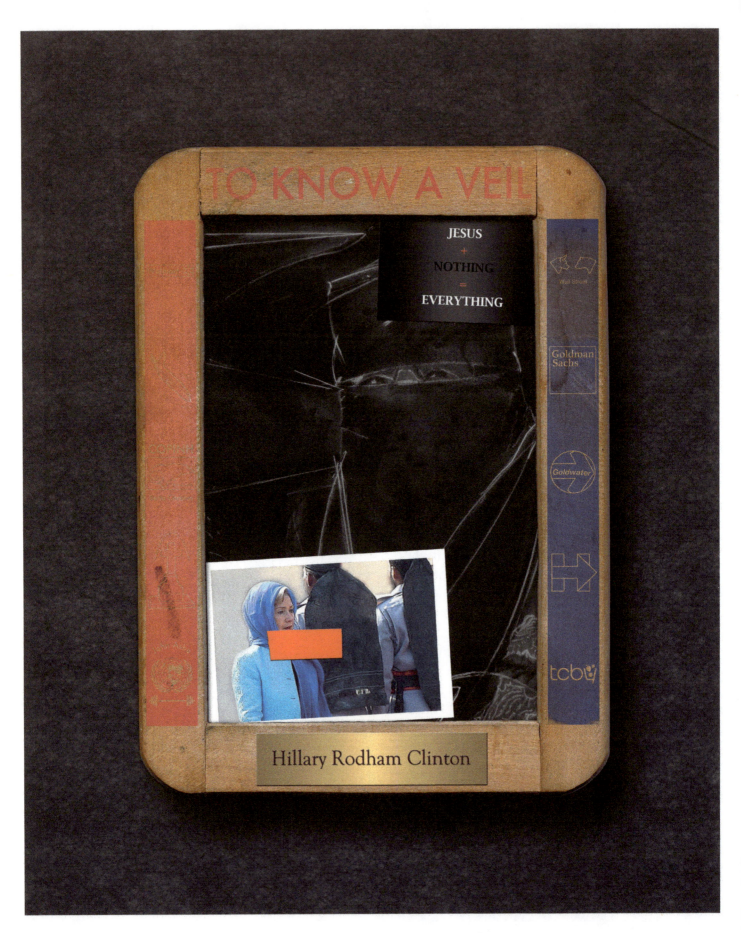

Plate 40

John A. O'Connor, *To Know Avail,* 2016-17. Digital Image, 21 x 17 in.

WHITE LIES MATTER

I'm very proud that I was a Goldwater Girl.[1]
—Hillary Rodham Clinton

Really? A Goldwater Girl! Hillary Rodham was born on October 26, 1947 in Chicago, Illinois to politically conservative parents. By the time she was thirteen, she was already working for Republican causes—looking for Democrat voter fraud in Chicago's South Side.[2]

Rodham's conservatism, at that time, was apparently shaped by her father and her high school history teacher, both staunch anti-communists, who introduced her to Barry Goldwater's political writings. She campaigned for Goldwater in the 1964 presidential campaign, but she did not vote for him. She was only sixteen.[3]

Following high school, she enrolled at Wellesley College, and, during her freshman year, was president of the Young Republicans. But, by her junior year, she had become a supporter of Democratic Presidential candidate Eugene McCarthy who wanted to end the Vietnam War. She also became a vocal advocate for civil rights. But then, she attended the 1968 Republican National convention.[4]

At this point in her life, it seems obvious that she had already established a pattern that her critics would label "flip-flops." Ironically, her senior thesis at Wellesley was on a Chicago community activist who would subsequently influence future president Barrack Obama. That thesis was suppressed by the Clinton White House and Wellesley College from 1993-2001—ostensibly because it exposed her radical views. That suppression was eventually described by her professor as "a stupid political decision, obviously, at the time."[5]

Following her graduation from Wellesley, she enrolled at Yale Law School because, although accepted at Harvard, a law professor there said, "We don't need any more women at Harvard."[6]

The rest is common knowledge. She campaigned for ultra-liberal George McGovern in 1972, then graduated from Yale Law in 1973. She had already been living with future husband William Jefferson Clinton for several years.

During this time, she gained a variety of legal experience. After failing to pass the bar exam for the District of Columbia but passing Arkansas', she began to teach law at the University of Arkansas. While there, she successfully defended a man accused of raping a twelve year old girl and then she helped to found a rape crisis hotline.[7] In October 1975, she married Bill Clinton. He was elected Arkansas' Attorney General in 1976, and they moved to Little Rock where she joined Rose Law Firm. During this time she was on the board of directors of TCBY, Wal-Mart, and Lafarge—all clients of Rose Law Firm.[8]

The Clinton's lives rapidly became frantic. Quickly flashing by were Whitewater Investment Corporation, Gennifer Flowers, Paula Jones, the "Stand By Your Man" insult of Tammy Wynette, Monica Lewinsky, the Fellowship, Health Care Reform, rejection of NAFTA, Travelgate, Vince Foster, Filegate, cattle futures controversy, missing White House gifts, the "vast right-wing conspiracy," USA PATRIOT Act, military action in Afghanistan, and Iraq, Benghazi, private email server, "dead broke" (the latter *Politifact* rates "Mostly False"), Goldman Sachs, Chelsea, outdrinking John McCain, love of Saudi Arabia. . . .

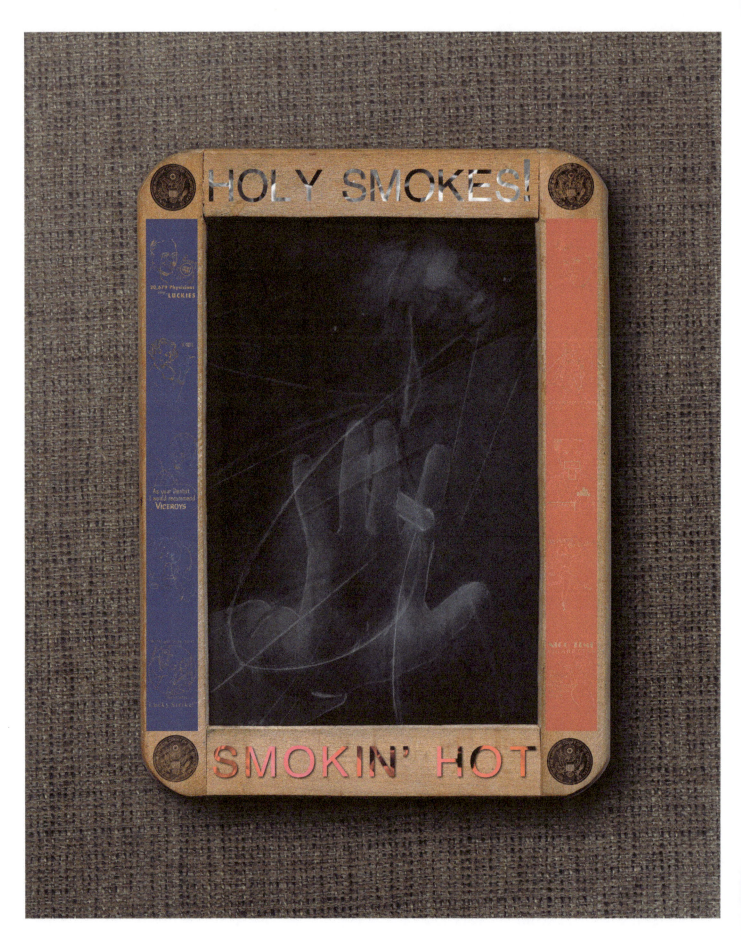

Plate 41

John A. O'Connor, *Smokin' Hot,* 2017-18. Digital Image, 21 x 17 in.

WHITE LIES MATTER

Cigarette smoking is no more addictive than coffee, tea or Twinkies.
    —James W. Johnston, CEO, RJR Nabisco[1]

The use of tobacco and tobacco products dates back to around 1 BCE, although it is thought that tobacco was growing in the Americas as early as 6,000 BCE.[2] It's earliest uses apparently were medicinal: it was used to cure everything, treat wounds, relieve pain, and stop toothaches.[3]

After Columbus "discovered" America and other early adventurers to the New World took the plant back to Europe, growing it rapidly spread throughout Europe. Europeans believed that it cured everything—including cancer and even bad breath![4] By 1571, a doctor in Spain claimed that tobacco could cure thirty-six diseases. Seventeen years later, tobacco was being promoted, in what would become Virginia, as a "viable way to get one's daily dose of tobacco" by the good Thomas Harriet—who, unfortunately, died of nose cancer. By the 1600s, tobacco had become "as good as gold." It, literally, was used as money, and by 1776, it helped finance the American Revolutionary War.

What about the other side of tobacco? Was the main ingredient in it a poison? Since nicotine wasn't discovered until 1826, who knew? Ten years later it was being used as an insecticide. (Kinda gives new meaning to the product called Reynolds Wrap!)[5]

But the real "explosion" of tobacco use occurred during World War I. It became known as the "soldiers smoke." But, since that was just for men, cigarette producers who obviously believed in women's equal rights, began marketing a product for women: a cigarette called "Mild as May." By the end of World War II, cigarette use was at an unsurpassed level having been included in C-Rations and provided for free to the soldiers.[6]

But by the 1950s, it appeared that there was a link between tobacco and lung cancer. Though that was vehemently denied by the industry, tobacco companies started to introduce low tar, and filtered cigarettes—one of which (Kent) had a "micronite" filter containing asbestos. By 1956, menthol-filtered cigarettes were introduced—perhaps to make one's breath smell fresher.

In 1964, the United States Surgeon General issued a report entitled "Smoking and Health." Two years later, warning notices on cigarette packs began, and major tobacco companies began removing the word "tobacco" from their name. American Tobacco Company became American Brands, Inc., RJ Reynolds Tobacco Company was renamed RJ Reynolds Industries (and they bought aluminum), Phillip Morris diversified and bought into the Miller Brewing Company. By 1971, cigarette ads were removed from television advertising. It wasn't until 1979, however, that the Surgeon General would issue a report on the consequences of smoking by women thus giving new meaning to the phrase, "You've Come a Long Way Baby!"[7] By 1985, lung cancer surpassed breast cancer as the number-one killer of women. Phillip Morris responded by acquiring shares of General Foods and Kraft. RJ Reynolds Industries further diversified and became RJR/ Nabisco. (Go Oreos!) By 1987, smoking began to be banned on U.S. airlines' domestic flights.

During this time, most of lawsuits brought against the tobacco companies were dismissed. But in February 2000, Philip Morris was ordered to pay $51.5 million to a Californian with lung cancer—the first major victory against tobacco companies. More than forty states sued the tobacco industry using antitrust and consumer protection laws and arguing that cigarettes caused significant health problems that cost the state public health systems a great amount of money. These lawsuits were also successful because the tobacco industry could not use the defense that had been so successful against individual smokers: that the smoker was aware of the risk and made the decision to smoke anyway.[8]

Plate 42
John A. O'Connor, *Falls Alarm,* 2016-17. Digital Image, 21 x 17 in.

WHITE LIES MATTER

It ain't as bad as you think. It will look better in the morning.[1]
—Colin Powell

The United States war in Iraq was partially based on manufactured "intelligence" that Iraqi President Sadam Hussein had WMD, or weapons of mass destruction. This action relied on "reports" from as early as 2001 that Hussein, in an attempt to rebuild Iraq's nuclear program, had attempted to buy "yellowcake" from Niger and several other countries. Although these reports were suspected by numerous intelligence agencies and many individuals to be fake, incomplete, or inaccurate, nevertheless they formed a significant part of the basis and justification of what then-President George W. Bush, aka "Dubya" relied on when making his decision to invade Iraq.[2]

But, far earlier, the groundwork for an invasion of Iraq was being laid. In 1993, it was reported that Saddam Hussein attempted to assassinate former President George H. W. Bush, Dubya's father. In October 1998, then-President Bill Clinton signed the Iraq Liberation Act making regime change there the official United States Policy. During this time Al Qaeda had bombed U.S. embassies in Africa and attacked U.S. assets elsewhere. By 2002, Vice President Cheney claimed that Saddam Hussein was pursuing nuclear weapons. The list of fabrications and lies went on and on, just like the war.[3]

By June 2002 the massive bombing of Iraq had begun although the war had not officially begun. And on February 5, 2003, Colin Powell told the United Nations that, "Every statement I make today is backed up by sources, solid sources. These are not assertions. What we're giving you are facts and conclusions based on solid intelligence." The war officially then began on March 20, 2003.[4]

Saying, "If you broke it, you own it," (the so-called "Pottery Barn rule") was Colin Powell's way of letting Dubya know about the potential consequences of a protracted war in Iraq. Ironically, even this is a lie. Michael Daley wrote in the New York Daily News on April 8, 2004, that Pow-

ell apparently picked up that saying from a baby furniture store he had worked at as a teenager.

The borders on this slate are images that can be interpreted in many ways—except for two of them. Can you find those images, and do you know what they represent? Hint: Their history begins toward the end of World War II.

And, by the way, since 1776, a number of sources (not necessarily credible but compelling nevertheless) claim that the United States has been at war for 224 of its 241 years of existence![5] And, at least one credible source says that the world has been at peace for "just 8 percent of recorded history."[6]

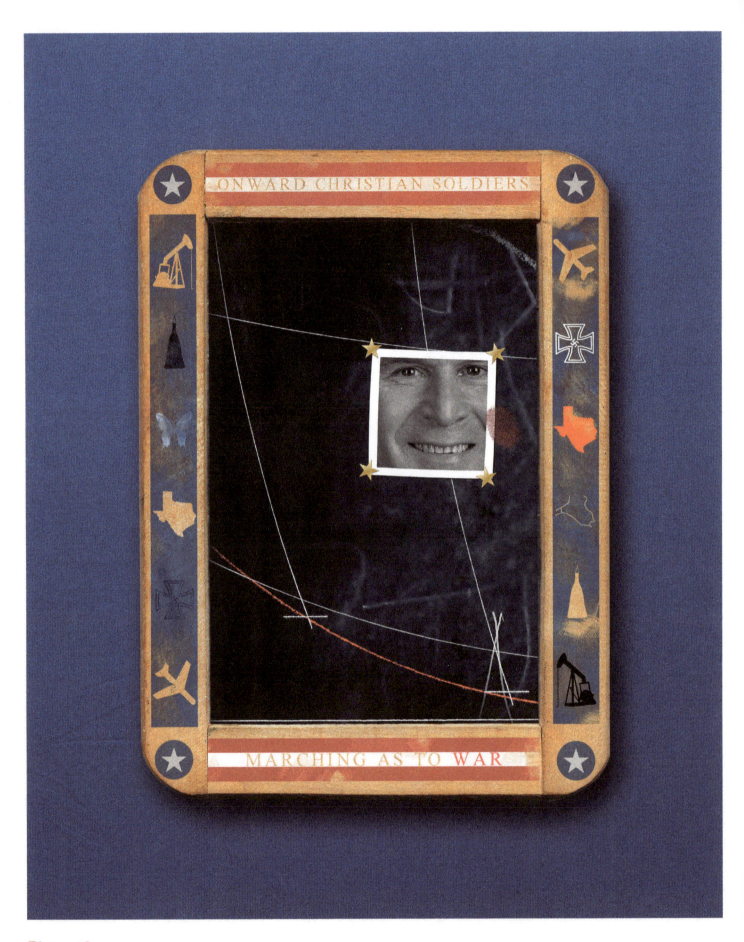

Plate 43
John A. O'Connor, *The Crusade,* 2016-17. Digital Image, 21 x 17 in.

WHITE LIES MATTER

I believe that God has planted in every human heart the desire to live in freedom. And even when that desire is crushed by tyranny for decades, it will rise again.[1]

George W. Bush's plans for war were very risky, but he was no gambler. He denied the existence of chance and even said, "Events aren't moved by blind change and chance" but by "the hand of a just and faithful God."

He was convinced that his presidency was part of a divine plan, even telling a friend while he was governor of Texas, "I believe God wants me to run for president," and his conviction that he was doing God's will surfaced openly after 9/11. The power of so-called "providentialist" thinking in the Bush administration persisted, drawing strength from the fervent beliefs of Christian, Islamic and Jewish fundamentalists.

The more humane interpreters of those traditions are increasingly ignored, and the ideologues take command, convinced that they are doing God's will.

Was Bush's crusade an extension of America's Manifest Destiny, a maneuver to find a new source of energy (oil), or was it really, as he insisted, a "liberating crusade in the Middle East," and "this call of history has come to the right country."

The term "crusade" describing the invasion of Iraq vanished almost as quickly as it was uttered. Clearly, however, Bush was guided by fundamentalist Christian views, just as his supporters insisted that "the rhetoric of Providence is as American as cherry pie."[2]

ONWARD CHRISTIAN SOLDIERS

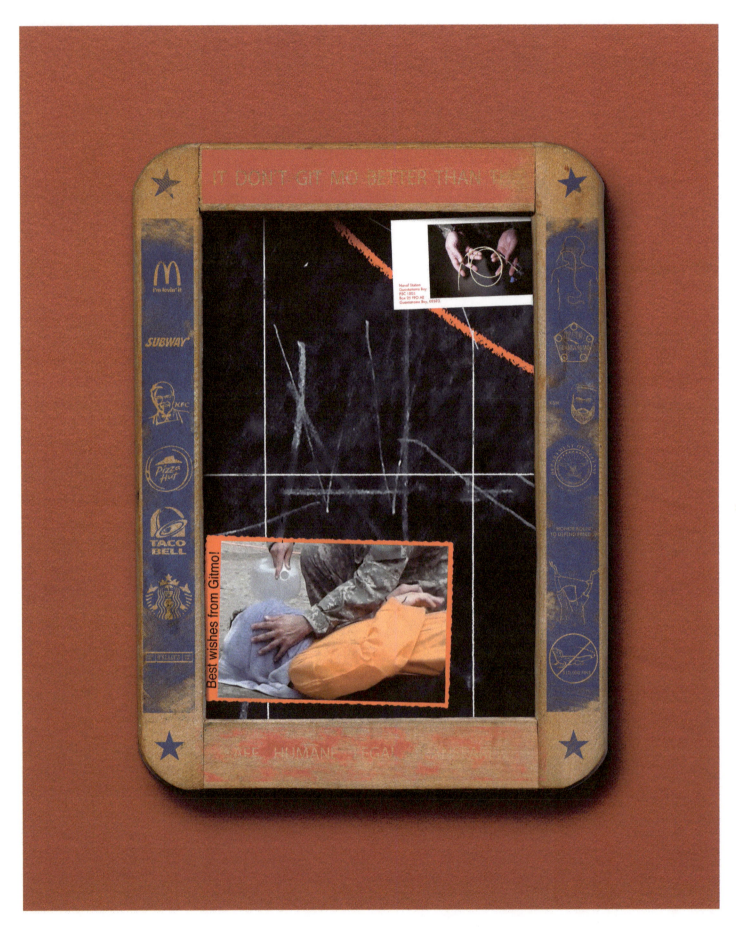

Plate 44
John A. O'Connor, *Gitmo,* 2016-17. Digital Image, 21 x 17 in.

WHITE LIES MATTER

122 vicious prisoners, released by the Obama Administration from Gitmo, have returned to the battlefield. Just another terrible decision![1]

The only thing wrong about Donald Trump's quote above is that, as the *Miami Herald* put it, "Trump blames wrong president for most Guantánamo 'back to battlefield' releases." The newspaper went on to state that, "Trump's vow to keep Guantánamo open and add new prisoners was a popular sound bite during his campaign."[2]

"Colonel Morris Davis, a staunch Guantánamo critic who served as the chief prosecutor at the detention facility, says the 'net result' between Bush and Obama is essentially the same. He characterizes the Bush administration 'as bad intentions coupled with a strong will in the face of no opposition.' The Obama administration, he says, is more a case of 'good intentions coupled with a weak will in the face of significant opposition.' "[3]

So, what is Guantánamo Bay? Established as a U.S. military prison in 2002, the U.S. has had complete control of this southeastern portion of Cuba since 1903 through a lease agreement for which the U.S. paid the Cuban government $2,000 a year. However, the U.S. first set up a navy base there in 1898 during the Spanish-American War. It houses the Bayview Restaurant, Bombers—a Mexican restaurant, Caribbean Coffee & Cream featuring Starbucks coffee, Pizza Hut, Spinz ("hand crafted food"), and the Windjammer.[4] A variety of alcoholic drinks are available at O'Kelly's Irish Pub, described as "the only Irish pub on Communist soil."[5] Was this actually the Military Fast-Food Industrial Complex?

The U.S. military website for Naval Station Guantánamo Bay, Cuba, states that the area population is 5,800.[6] **It currently houses forty-one prisoners at an estimated cost of $10.8 million per prisoner per year.**[7]

Referred to by many as the Pearl of the Antilles, Gitmo as it is commonly known, has a number of what can only be described as peculiar attributes. It is the sole American military base in a communist country. Killing an iguana can set you back $10,000. With a Mr. and Mrs. Gitmo Figure and Fitness Competition, and an in-house magazine called, appropriately, the *Wire,* movie theaters and restaurants, a Zombie 5K run, a Sure Start-12 educational system, it has been dubbed the typical U.S. suburb.[8]

Naval Station
Guantanamo Bay
PSC 1005
Box 25 FPO AE
Guantanamo Bay, 09593

IT DON'T GIT MO BETTER THAN T

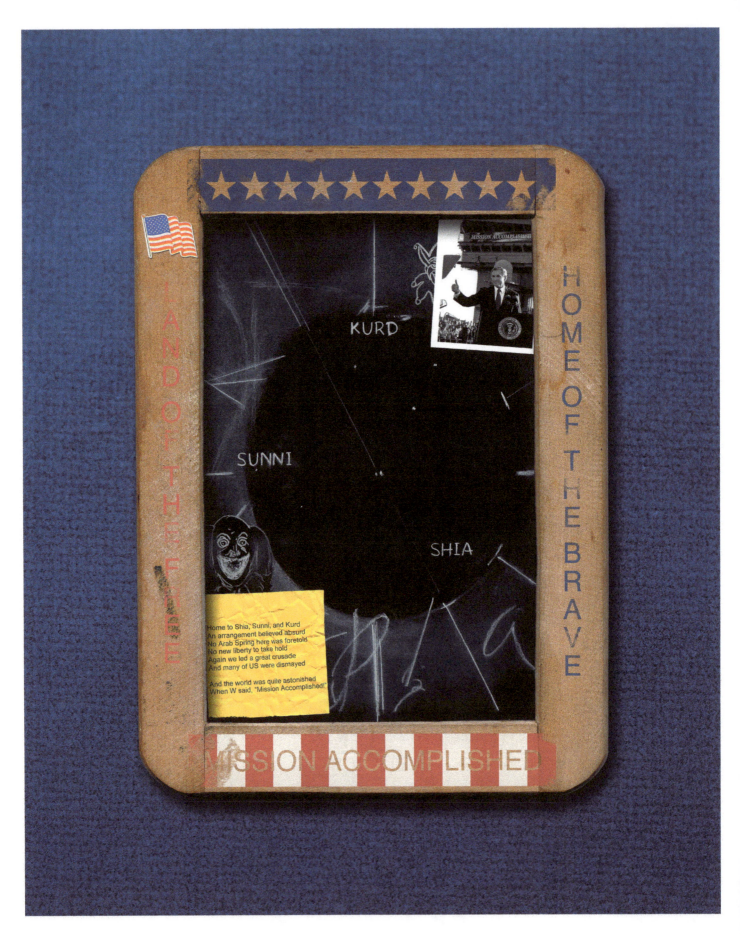

Plate 45
John A. O'Connor, *Poetic Justice,* 2016-17. Digital Image, 21 x 17 in.

WHITE LIES MATTER

MISSION ACCOMPLISHED

English drama critic Thomas Rymer coined the phrase "poetic justice" in *The Tragedies of the Last Age Considere'd* (1678) to describe how a work should inspire proper moral behavior in its audience by illustrating the triumph of good over evil.[1]

George W. Bush's 2003 "Mission Accomplished" speech got its name from the banner that was displayed on the aircraft carrier USS Abraham Lincoln. It triumphantly (and blatantly) announced that the U.S. mission in Iraq had been accomplished. It occurred during a televised address by United States President Bush on May 1, 2003. The controversy followed.[2]

Bush's "prophetic pronouncement" of "Mission Accomplished" certainly gives the title of this work *Poetic Justice* a new twist. The slate image contains a 'black hole' surrounded by an image of a clown and a joker. The words Shia, Sunni, and Kurd are

written on the slate. Their fate is discussed in the "post-it" poem that I wrote in syllabic verse.

Francis Scott Key wrote "the land of the free and the home of the brave" in 1814. Since 1931, it has been sung as the national anthem of the United States.[3] Ironically, Key was a slave-holder, and the U.S. wars in the middle–East have been, correctly portrayed, many believe, as racist/religious wars.

Mission Accomplished.

Many years later. . . .

REALLY?

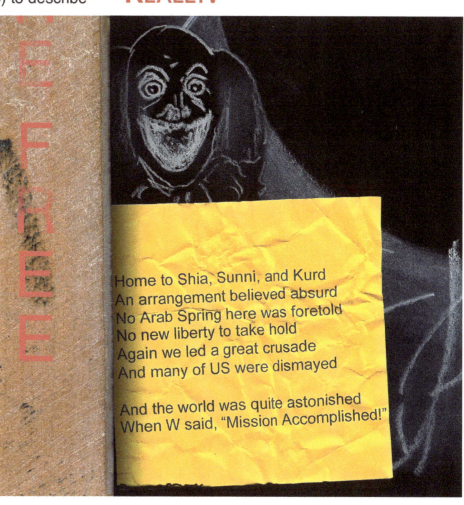

Home to Shia, Sunni, and Kurd
An arrangement believed absurd
No Arab Spring here was foretold
No new liberty to take hold
Again we led a great crusade
And many of US were dismayed

And the world was quite astonished
When W said, "Mission Accomplished!"

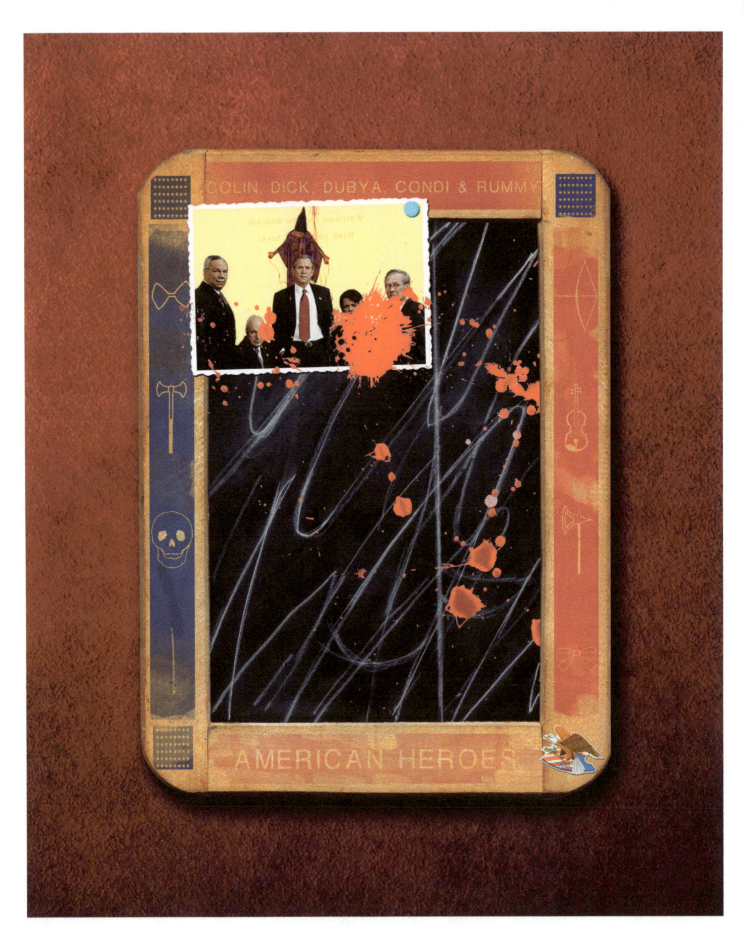

Plate 46
John A. O'Connor, *Violin Tax?,* 2016-17. Digital Image, 21 x 17 in.

WHITE LIES MATTER

The treatment of those detained at Abu Ghraib is governed by the Geneva Conventions, which have been signed by both the U.S. and Iraq.[1]

According to many accounts during 2004, numerous acts of horrendous violence and violation of human rights were committed by U.S. Army soldiers and the U.S. Central Intelligence Agency (CIA) during the war that began in Iraq in 2003. Torture, rape, sodomy, even murder—you name it, and it probably occurred under the watch of the U.S. government officials pictured in the "post-card" in this slate, *Violin Tax.*

The abuses were originally portrayed by these officials and others as isolated, unsanctioned incidents although subsequent investigation revealed that they were approved by Donald Rumsfeld, then-Secretary of Defense. While official U.S. policymakers insisted that these crimes were infrequent, it was subsequently revealed that they took place not only at Abu Ghraib prison in Iraq, but also occurred in Afghanistan, and also at America's military base at Guantánamo Bay, Cuba.

It was not generally known during this time that the U.S. government had justified "enhanced interrogation" as a legal way to obtain information from so-called "enemy combatants," because, according to the U.S. Department of Justice, these enemy combatants were not covered by the Geneva Convention. Known as the "Torture Memos," these incredible legal interpretations were written by John Yoo, a Deputy Assistant Attorney General of the United States. What makes this more surprising is that Yoo, a native-born South Korean, held degrees in law from Yale and Harvard Universities, served, since 1993, as a professor of law at the University of California at Berkeley and subsequently served at a number of other universities and think tanks.

Who was responsible for the torture at Abu Ghraib? Well, the individuals pictured in *Violin Tax* were never charged, indicted, or prosecuted. But, one Janis Karpinski, a U.S. Brigadier General who was in charge of all U.S. military prisons in Iraq—even though she had absolutely no experience running a prison, let alone prisons– was eventually demoted to the rank of Colonel. How ironic that a number of lower level military women also participated in the torture and sexual humiliation of the prisoners at Abu Ghraib? And, the blood spatters? Yes, violent, bloody murders were carried out by U.S. soldiers there.[2]

AMERICAN HEROES anyone?

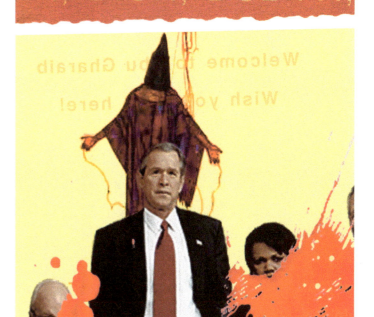

Plate 47
John A. O'Connor, *Concealed Kerry,* 2016-17. Digital Image, 21 x 17 in.

WHITE LIES MATTER

"You know, education, if you make the most of it, if you study hard and do your homework, and you make an effort to be smart, you can do well." But, he added, "If you don't, you get stuck in Iraq."[1]

John Kerry made those remarks to students at Pasadena City College on October 31, 2006, while campaigning for a colleague. Relatively simple and straightforward on first reading, they mask the identity of a person who is quite different from his well-known public persona.

Although John Kerry was born in Colorado, his full name is John Forbes Kerry. He is a member of that well-known, wealthy Irish family from Boston, Massachusetts. His extended family includes the very wealthy Winthrop clan.[2] Raised as a Irish-Catholic, he served as an altar boy.[3]

However, the Kerry family name actually was Kohn. John Forbes Kerry's father was Austrian, and his mother was Hungarian. Both were Jews. The name "Kerry" apparently came about when a family member dropped a pencil on a map of Ireland, and it just happened to land on County Kerry. John Forbes Kerry claims that he did not learn about this until 2003.[4]

Interestingly, Kerry who many people believe to be a highly intelligent and well-educated person received lower grades at Yale than the much maligned and often derided "stupid" George W. Bush. "I always told my Dad that D stood for distinction," he said about all of the D grades he received.[5] Yet, Kerry apparently was an excellent debater and won many debates against students from across America. He also was described as an excellent orator.[6]

Like his opponent George W. Bush in the 2004 U.S. presidential election, Kerry also went to Yale University, and like Dubya he became a Bonesman—a member of Yale's infamous secret society. Supposedly, John Kerry's Skull and Bones nickname was Long Devil, although some dispute this and suggest that name was reserved for the tallest Bonesman. But since the society is "secret," and Kerry himself wouldn't say more than, "I wish there were something secret I could

manifest there,"[7] it is impossible to verify the accuracy of this description.

John Kerry's current wife, Teresa Heinz Kerry is a very rich woman whose previous husband, H. John Heinz III was also a U.S. senator and, coincidentally, his father was also a member of Skull and Bones.[8]

Kerry's military career in Vietnam is surrounded by significant controversy. A group of his colleagues calling themselves Swift Boat Veterans for Truth said that Kerry was not qualified to receive the three Purple Hearts, Bronze Star Medal, and Silver Star awarded to him. Other who served with Kerry deny the claims of the Swift Boat Veterans for Truth.[9] Ironically, the continuing attack on Kerry's activities on the Swift Boat is known today as "swiftboating"—a term that many would say defines a white lie, or worse.[10]

When Kerry returned from Vietnam following a four-month tour of duty, he joined the Vietnam Veterans Against the War, and subsequently threw away his medals. Or did he? Controversy on this issue continues today because Kerry himself has told numerous versions of what really happened to his medals, or ribbons, or whatever they were.[11]

In 2004, Kerry also severely criticized President Bush for U.S. involvement in the Iraq War, yet he voted for it in 2002. On March 16, 2004, regarding a supplemental appropriations bill for the Iraq War, Kerry said he "actually did vote for the $87 billion before I voted against it."[12]

Plate 48

John A. O'Connor, *Blood Libel,* 2016-17. Digital Image, 21 x 17 in.

WHITE LIES MATTER

"Journalists and pundits should not manufacture a blood libel. . . ."[1]

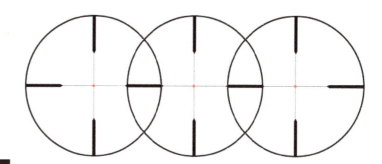

Democrat Congresswoman Gabrielle Giffords was brutally shot by Jared Lee Loughner in a murderous onslaught against a crowd attending her meeting of constituents near Tucson, Arizona, on January 8, 2011. Of the nineteen people injured, six died.

At that time, Sara Palin was vigorously campaigning for her 2008 partner, Arizona Senator John McCain. Also playing a prominent role in this happy version of Tea Party politics was Janice Brewer, then-Governor of Arizona—the state ranked number one for gun owners.[2]

What most people didn't know when Palin uttered her infamous "blood libel" comment was that Giffords was Arizona's first Jewish Congresswoman. So, what of it?

So, what of "bomb, bomb Iran," John McCain's famous mantra in the 2008 election? Think about it. McCain choose Palin to be his Vice Presidential running mate. Both were supported by Governor Brewer. McCain is not only a known, military hawk and avid gun rights supporter, but also he has received more money from the National Rifle Association than any politician in

American history! How fitting is it then, that McCain blamed former President Obama for the mass shooting at a gay nightclub in Orlando, Florida?

It is also common knowledge, that during the 2012 campaign, Palin was roundly criticized for marking districts with cross hairs that the Republicans sought to take back.

So, what is blood libel? Does it refer to the crucifixion of Jesus by the Jews as some Christians contend? Mentioned in Matthew 27:25, it has often been interpreted that way.[3]

Usually, blood libel is described as an inhuman act involving Jews kidnapping and murdering children in order to use their blood in ritual religious practices—or in their food (as in matzo and wine) although it is prohibited by the teachings of Judaism. Described as a horrible practice, it has been attributed throughout history by many as a particularly Jewish practice. Catholics and Muslims have frequently derided Jews for this heinous act.[4]

Numerous defenders of Sarah Palin, both on the left and right, have concluded that she may not have really understood what the phrase "blood libel" actually means. Palin has, of course, routinely criticized the press for inaccurately and savagely attacking her for using the term. She has also routinely attacked journalists for many other things. Ironically (or is it coincidentally?), Palin was born a Catholic who then converted to Pentecostalism, and is a graduate of the University of Idaho with a **degree in communications with an emphasis in journalism!**

Plate 49
John A. O'Connor, *Patriotic Assets,* 2016-17. Digital Image, 21 x 17 in.

WHITE LIES MATTER

What does that gold star mean?

The images represented in the panels symbolize some of the materials, means, and methods used by so-called "intelligence agencies" to obtain information on residents of various countries.

Espionage, or spying, of course is nothing new. Even many of the methods depicted in the slate, *Patriotic Assets,* to obtain intel are historic. Notice the number of images on each panel, add them up, then compare that number to the of spies who entered the so-called "Promised Land." Yes, you may need to refer to the "Old Testa-

ment" of the Bible or the Hebrew Bible.

Actually, spying is even more ancient than that! It probably is at least as old as the so-called oldest profession. And, it has been common in almost all cultures

However, some of the images depict relatively recent inventions.

There is also a silhouette of a famous person who is the subject of a great deal of recent discussion about legal and illegal "monitoring," and "surveillance." Most of the current in-depth searches of U.S. citizens (and others) are made possible by the ironically named Patriot Act.

"The president also knows from the NSA's damage assessment that Snowden compromised materials critical in the intelligence war against Russia, including documents NSA Deputy Director Richard Ledgett called the 'keys to the kingdom.' "[2] Interestingly, "keys to the kingdom" is the title of a recent book by former U.S. Senator Bob Graham of Florida—and "keys of the kingdom" is "a Christian concept of eternal church authority."[3]

FACE OF INTELLIGENCE

Plate 50

John A. O'Connor, *Beneath the Pale,* 2016-17. Digital Image, 21 x 17 in.

WHITE LIES MATTER

"Everybody is comparing the oil spill to Hurricane Katrina, but the real parallel could be the Iranian hostage crisis. In the late 1970s, the hostage crisis became a symbol of America's inability to take decisive action in the face of pervasive problems. In the same way, the uncontrolled oil plume could become the objective correlative of the country's inability to govern itself."[1]

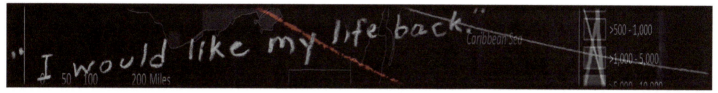

Would you believe that a conservative Republican who once wrote for the *Wall Street Journal* made the quote above? And, ironically, why did he equate this disaster with Iran? Was he prescient, or did he simply do his homework?

It has been more than eight years since the Deepwater Horizon rig exploded on April 20, 2010, in the Gulf of Mexico and created the largest offshore oil disaster in history. Eleven workers died while some 210 million gallons of oil poured into the Gulf of Mexico, at least 1,400 dolphins died, and estimates suggest that at least 1,000,000 birds were killed. How did this happen and who was responsible?

In 1908, the British Anglo-Persian Oil Company (APOC) began extracting oil from Iran. In 1935, it was renamed the Anglo-Iranian Oil Company (AIOC). In 1954 it was renamed again. This time it became BP, the British Petroleum Company[2]—the company responsible for this great disaster known variously as the Deepwater Horizon Oil Spill, the BP Oil Spill, or the Macondo Incident—among many other, perhaps even less flattering names.[3]

The number of fingers in this pie is herculean. BP chartered the rig that was built by Hyundai Heavy Industries, owned by Transocean, and it was being operated under a "flag of convenience" of the Marshall Islands. To complicate this further, BP had a 65% share in the project, Andarko Petroleum Corporation had a 25%

share, and MOEX Offshore 2007 held a 10% share—the last one a subsidiary of Mitsui which probably no one has ever heard of even though it is one of the world's largest corporate entities. Halliburton, another of the world's largest corporations linked to this incident because of its role in "the cement job it did to seal BP 's Macondo oil well," paid out over $1.1 bullion—even though it denied any blame or responsibility in this debacle.[4]

This catastrophe of monumental proportions was dubbed "the world's largest accidental release of oil into marine waters. . . ."[5]

Accidental? Then why did BP subsequently plead guilty to eleven counts of manslaughter, two misdemeanors, and lying to Congress—a felony. Subsequently, BP also was subjected to unprecedented government monitoring, and EPA banned it from competing for new contracts with the U.S. government. By February 2013, it had reportedly cost BP over $42 billion. Additionally, in July of 2015, BP agreed to pay more than $18 billion in fines.[6] But by October 2015, that number had risen to $20.8 billion—the largest penalty for **accidental** pollution in U.S. History.[7] [Emphasis added.]

Just how extensive was this accidental oil spill? Well, it washed up on the shores of Texas, Louisiana, Mississippi, Alabama, and Florida. Oil was found along 1,313 miles of these shorelines.[8] The numbers of endangered wildlife. . .

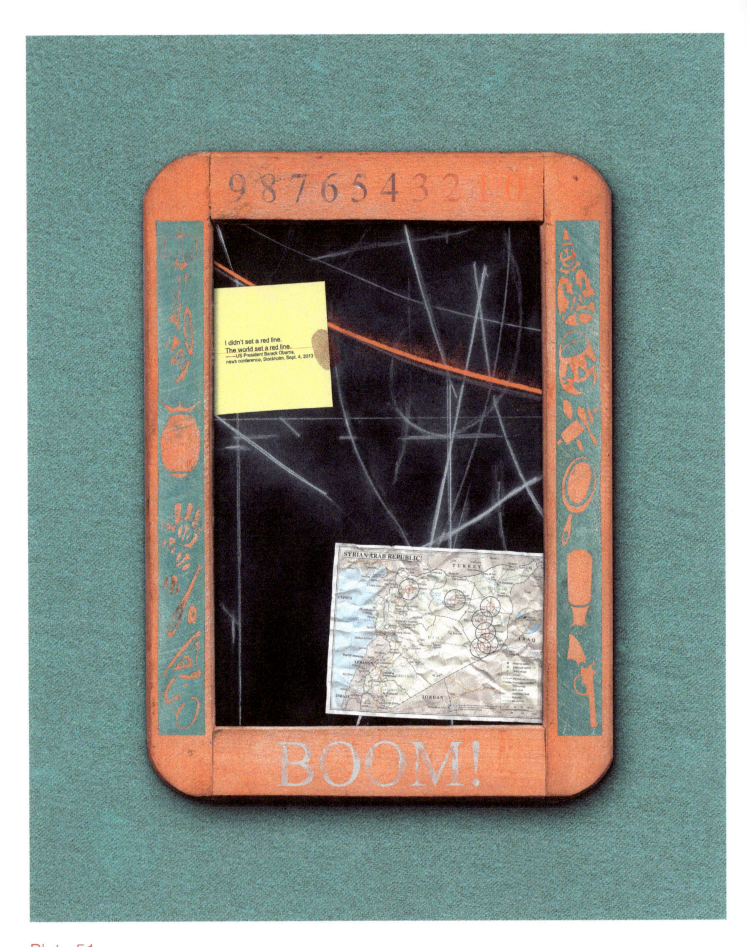

Plate 51
John A. O'Connor, *The Continuing Crusade,* 2016-17. Digital Image, 21 x 17 in.

WHITE LIES MATTER

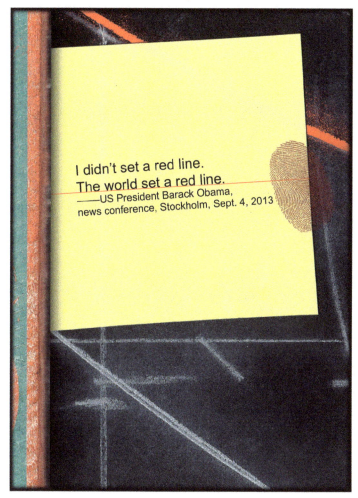

I didn't set a red line.
The world set a red line.
——US President Barack Obama,
news conference, Stockholm, Sept. 4, 2013

Barack Obama's comment that he didn't set a red line strikes many as a peculiar retreat from him saying just that. Glenn Kessler on September 6, 2013, wrote in *The Washington Post* that "a red line" has been rhetorically troublesome for the president ever since he uttered those words about a year ago. . . ."

Many pundits and journalists would have happily rewarded the president with "Pinocchios" for his ambiguous interpretation and subsequent reinterpretation of the facts about the war in Syria, and also his own reinvention and reinterpretation of his own remarks. Indeed, his entire administration got in on this act—particularly when then-Secretary of State John Kerry reiterated that it was the world's red line.

The numbers at the top obviously refer to the "countdown" to "BOOM," which is depicted by the target on the "wrinkled map" of Syria—targets that the American Air Force apparently did bomb.

The left and right panels (i.e. border decoration) are original to an actual slate with the exception of two updated symbols of American violence in World War II. Can you find them? What do they represent?

Oh, and the red line and the "bloody fingerprint." I wonder what they could represent?

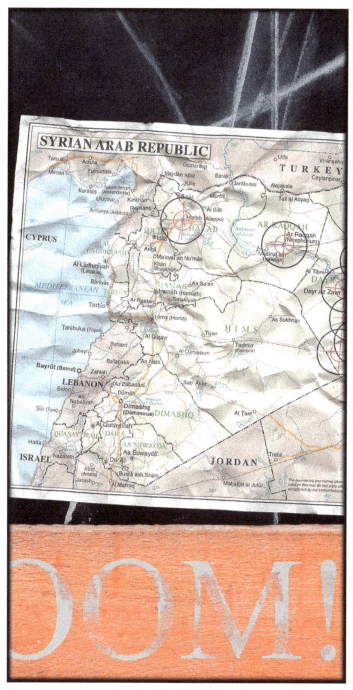

Plate 52

John A. O'Connor, *The Caged Bird Sings,* 2016-17. Digital Image, 21 x 17 in.

WHITE LIES MATTER

A bird doesn't sing because it has an answer, it sings because it has a song.[1]
—Maya Angelou

It has been repeatedly said that pretty much anyone could be forgiven for thinking that the quote above was originated by the late poet Maya Angelou, who wrote *I Know Why the Caged Bird Sings*. But did she write it? And, if not, why did President Obama attribute it to her when he used these words in his opening remarks at the 2013 National Medals of the Arts and Humanities presentation? And, if the quote is not something that Maya Angelou said, who did? And why does it matter? Isn't it just a mistake or a "little white lie"?

Not only did President Obama credit Angelou with the quote, but it also showed up on April 7, 2015 on a U.S. "Forever" postage stamp along with her portrait taken from an oil painting by Russ Rossin that is in the collection of the Smithsonian National Portrait Gallery.[2]

The quote actually belongs to Joan Walsh Anglund, an author of children's books, who wrote it in her 1967 book, *A Cup of Sun*. Anglund's version does vary slightly in that "it" is "he" in the original. Ironically, the U.S. Postal Service initially defended its plagiarism by claiming that it had been attributed by everyone to Angelou. It even went on to say, "The Postal Service used her widely recognized quote to help build an immediate connection between her image and her 1969 nationally recognized autobiography, 'I Know Why the Caged Bird Sings,'" spokesman Mark Saunders said.[3]

Many people will consider this situation irrelevant or even laughable. But is it? Is plagiarism irrelevant? Does it have no consequences? *The Law Dictionary* says, "Copying someone else's work and passing it off as one's own can come with serious consequences. Some of these are personal, some are professional and some are legal. These consequences can vary depending upon how and where the plagiarism occurred." It goes on to note, "When a professional commits plagiarism, the stakes are even higher. Notoriety as a plagiarist can effectively end a career. The plagiarist may be asked to leave their job or be fired."[4]

Of course, there also can be legal consequences. But when one examines the list of well-known journalists or politicians who have been accused of plagiarism, it appears that most of them have avoided any real punishment.

Ironically, the only person I know who suffered any consequences for plagiarism was fired. He was a local school superintendent who just happened to be black.

Historically, some famous people have been cited for plagiarism. They include Dr. Martin Luther King, Jr. whose doctoral dissertation and other writings were taken from non-attributed sources. Scientist Jane Goddall has been accused of lifting material from *Wikipedia*. Even Johnny Cash, the famous country music star, was sued over supposedly stealing the lyrics and music of "Folsom Prison Blues" from a 1953 song by Gordon Jenkins. Others involved in plagiarism issues include the Beach Boys, George Harrison, Led Zeppelin, and Hellen Keller—a 1961 recipient of the Presidential Medal of Freedom. Arguably one of the best known of all of the plagiarists was T. S. Elliot, the Nobel Prize winning poet. And, so we have come full circle.[5]

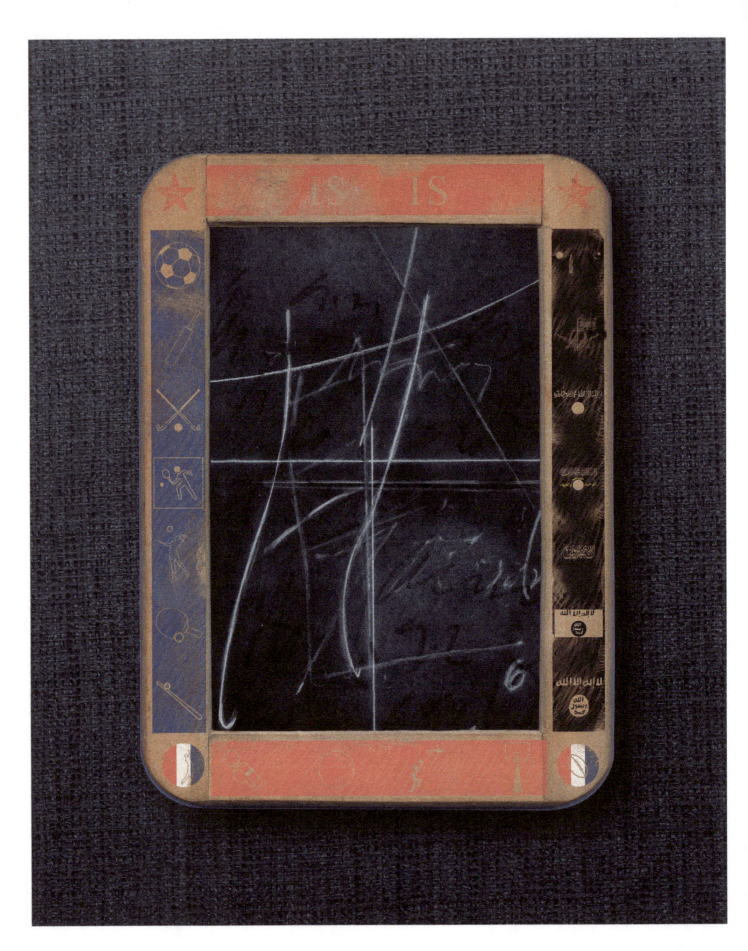

Plate 53

John A. O'Connor, *The Junior Varsity,* 2017. Digital Image, 21 x 17 in.

WHITE LIES MATTER

"The label Junior Varsity made sense from the perspective of what they had accomplished at the time."[1]

Did President Barack Obama really refer to ISIS (or ISIL, or Daesh—an acronym for Islamic State of Iraq and the Levant) as the junior varsity? Well, in an article in *The New Yorker,* he is quoted as saying, "The analogy we use around here sometimes, and I think is accurate, is if a jayvee team puts on Lakers uniforms that doesn't make them Kobe Bryant." The then-White House Press Secretary subsequently "clarified" Obama's remark by stating that the President's comment was taken out of context. [How convenient!] That clarification won the Press Secretary "four Pinocchios"—*The Washington Post's* worst rating.[2] Obama said subsequently, "Keep in mind I wasn't specifically referring to ISIL"[3] Kind of reminds me of the red line in Syria that President Obama didn't say either.

How ironic is it that President Obama chose Kobe Bryant as the symbol of the LA Lakers. Famous Lakers such as Bryant, Shaquille O'Neal,[4] and Magic Johnson[5] all have rather sordid sexual histories. Why not pick Kareem Abdul-Jabar—a highly respected former Laker and currently a well-respected journalist and businessman—among many other noteworthy achievements? Was it because Jabar is a Muslim? Just asking? After all, Obama awarded him the Presidential Medal of Freedom in 2016!

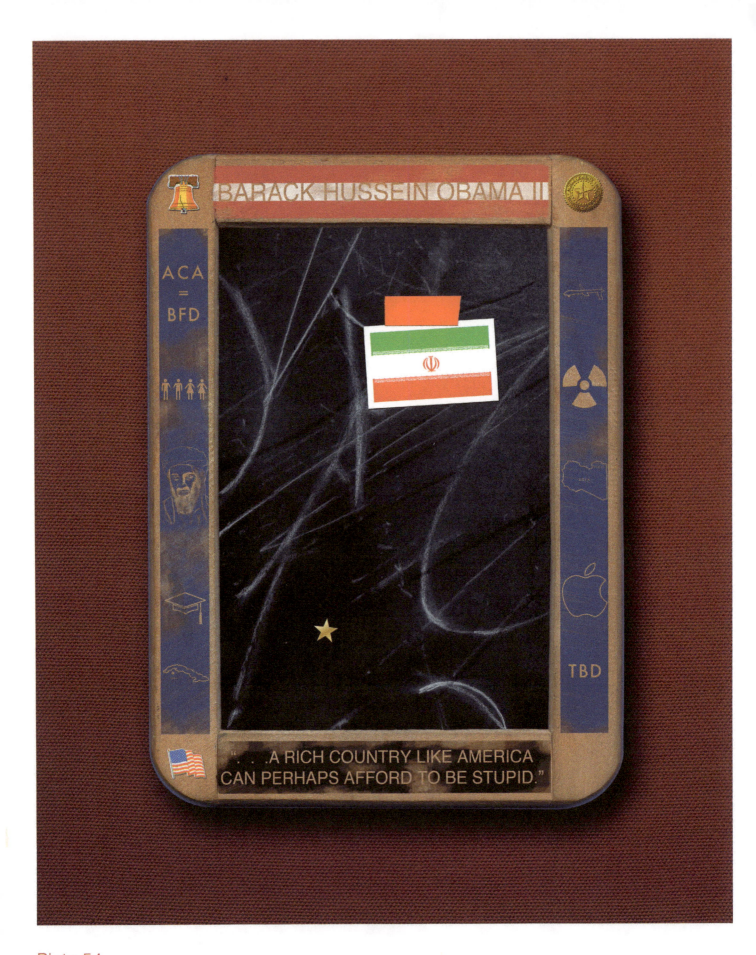

Plate 54

John A. O'Connor, *The Legacy,* 2017. Digital Image, 21 x 17 in.

WHITE LIES MATTER

"Let's compare Barack Obama with his predecessor. Whatever legitimate criticisms of George W. Bush's foreign policy one can make—and we made many contemporaneously and would still make many—let's be clear: Bush basically succeeded."[1]

While many historians probably believe that it may be far too soon to judge President Barack Obama's presidency, it hasn't stopped pundits like William Kristol from scathing criticism such as "Indeed the real question about the Obama legacy probably should be: Has America ever had a worse foreign policy president? We can't think of who that would be."[2]

On the other hand, Michael Grunwald seems to think, as Joe Biden notoriously said, when speaking of Obamacare (the Affordable Care Act–ACA) that it was a BFD.[3] He goes on to say, "What he's done is changing the way we produce and consume energy, the way doctors and hospitals treat us, the academic standards in our schools and the long-term fiscal trajectory of the nation. Gays can now serve openly in the military, insurers can no longer deny coverage because of pre-existing conditions, credit card companies can no longer impose hidden fees and markets no longer believe the biggest banks are too big to fail. Solar energy installations are up nearly 2,000 percent, and carbon emissions have dropped even though the economy is growing."[4]

Laura Belmonte, Professor and Head of the History Department at Oklahoma State University says, "Throughout his presidency, Barack Obama's extraordinary capacity to tap people's deepest aspirations collided with domestic political divides that severely limited his ability to build an enduring legislative program comparable to the New Deal, the Great Society, or the Reagan revolution."[5]

H. W. Brands, Professor of History at the University of Texas at Austin says, "The single undeniable aspect of Obama's legacy is that he demonstrated that a black man can become president of the United States. This accomplishment will inform the first line in his obituary and will earn him assured mention in every American history textbook written from now to eternity.

For all else, it's too soon to tell."[6]

Doris Kearns Goodwin, presidential historian says, "In the near-term, he brought stability to the economy, to the job market, to the housing market, to the auto industry and to the banks. That's what he's handing over: an economy that is in far better form than it was when he took over. And you can also say he'll be remembered for his dignity, grace, and the lack of scandal. And then the question is in the longer term what have you left for the future that will be remembered by historians years from now. Some of that will depend on what happens to health care."[7]

Then, there is Glass-Steagall and Dodd-Frank, Iran and Israel. U.S. Cyber command, renewal of the Patriot Act, Cuban-American relations thawing, Guantánamo still operating, Libya unsettled, Osama bin Laden killed, Syria still at war, Iraq a mess, Afghanistan still unsettled, and who knows about his environmental executive orders and The Paris Agreement on climate change, or the Iran Nuclear Deal, "If you like your doctor, you'll be able to keep him," same sex marriage. . . .

Plate 55

John A. O'Connor, *TrumpupPence,* 2017. Digital Image, 21 x 17 in.

WHITE LIES MATTER

Vice-President Mike Pence—a hard-line evangelical who has repeatedly called himself "a Christian, a conservative, and a Republican, in that order"—refuses to dine extramaritally. If he eats alone with a woman, that woman is Karen Pence; if he attends an event where alcohol is served and "people are being loose," he prefers that his wife be present and standing close to him.[1]

He is the man who has been described as "the de facto leader of the Republican party, which is no longer the party of conservatism but is now the party of nationalism; but more importantly Mike Pence is at the head of another, far more dangerous Republican group, the 'Christian Supremacists.' "[2]

Pence was born into an Irish Catholic family. He was both a Roman Catholic and a Democrat. He even voted for Jimmy Carter in 1980 over the great Republican Ronald Reagan.[3] He got into politics because John F. Kennedy and Martin Luther King Jr. inspired him.[4]

Who are his heroes? Beside Jesus, they include Ronald Reagan and Rush Limbaugh. But his most important hero "was evangelist James Dobson" whose invitation to appear on his (Dobson's) radio show caused Pence to gleefully announce that "being interviewed by Dobson 'was the greatest honor of my entire life.' "[5] Pence went on to host his own radio show, "The Mike Pence Show" that was syndicated to eighteen Indiana radio stations. As the show reached more and more listeners, Pence's political career was significantly reinvigorated.

Sandy Hook Elementary and same-sex marriage. Same-sex marriage will cause a new Civil War? (How civil is war, anyway?) Those are Dobson's views and he is Pence's hero.

What is Mike Pence's connection to the "Alt Right"? Is it Stephen Bannon? Richard Spencer? White nationalism? White Supremacy? Nazi ideology? Is there really a connection between white supremacy, the KKK, and the Nazis?

"Sexual behavior is the main plank in the broad platform supporting the new Republican party and particularly the Christian alt-right under the loving guidance of religious fanatic Mike Pence and his friends and mentors in the evangelical/televangelical world."[6]

According to Ursula Faw, and many others, all of this movement toward the extreme religious right began in earnest during Ronald Reagan's first term as president. Pat Robertson spoke out against pluralism, Billy Graham announced, "I'm for evangelicals 'getting control of the Congress, getting control of the bureaucracy, getting control of the executive branch of government. If we leave it to the other side we're going to be lost.' "[7] Tim LaHaye and Phyllis Schlafly proposed the same ideas.

Media clearly was a boon to the evangelical-political movement as Pat Robertson's TV program, the 700 Club, was at the top of Nielsen ratings in 1985.[8]

Subsequently, Pence became a friend of Erik Prince, a former Navy SEAL and founder of Blackwater, a security company sometimes referred to as a mercenary militia probably because of its murder of seventeen Iraqi citizens in Baghdad in 2007.[9] Prince is currently considering running for the U.S. Senate as a Republican in Wyoming with the backing of Stephen Bannon.[10] Prince's family funded the Family Research Council and James Dobson's Focus on the Family. His sister is Betsy DeVos, the current U.S. Secretary of Education. Apparently, they were also friends of Charles Colson—the first of Richard Nixon's Watergate conspirators to be sentenced.[11]

If, in the next few years, "Make America Great Again" begets "Make America Christian Again," Pence and his cohorts will have succeeded in doing precisely what they scream against—making the United States into the Christian equivalent of Iran—a Christian Caliphate.

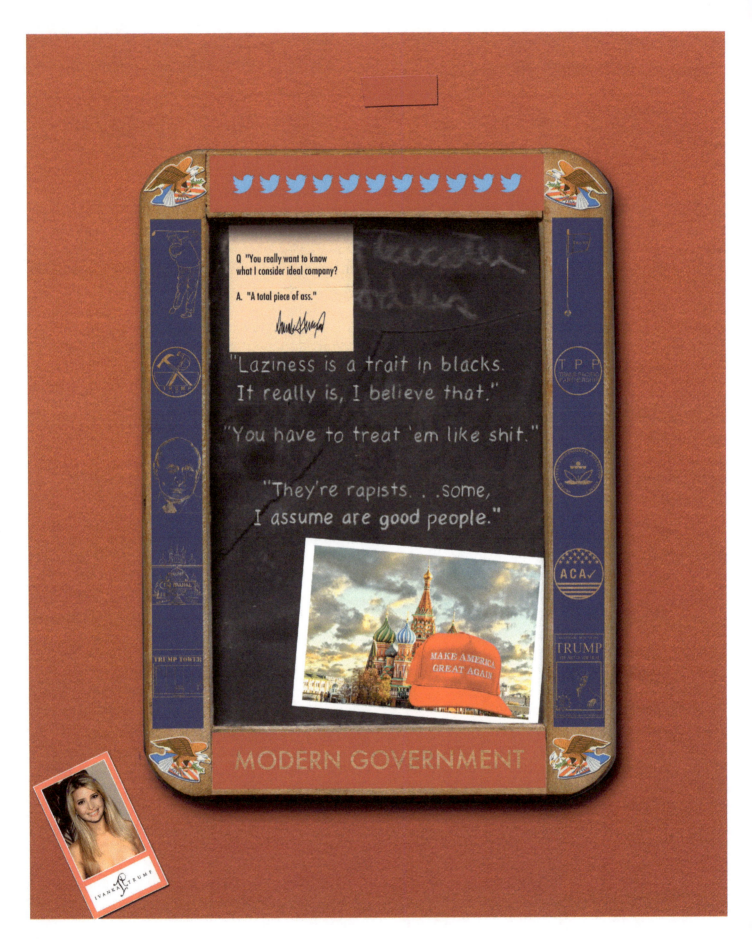

Plate 56

John A. O'Connor, *Ill Eagle,* 2017-18. Digital Image, 21 x 17 in.

W<small>HITE</small> L<small>IES</small> M<small>ATTER</small>

Donald John Trump, the 45th president of the United States, a real estate mogul and former reality television star, is also a supposed billionaire. I say supposed because no one—except maybe those in his inner circle—really knows. He was the only major-party presidential candidate since Gerald Ford not to release at least one income tax form.[1]

Trump was a very successful TV show host of *The Apprentice* for fourteen seasons even though he had initially told producer Mark Burnett that reality television "was for the bottom feeders of society."[2]

But, as a businessman, prior to becoming president, he probably was best known for Trump Tower, the Taj Mahal, Trump Castle, and Mar-a-Lago, a Florida estate in Palm Beach.

He is also well known for his comment on John McCain. "He's not a war hero. He's a war hero because he was captured. I like people who weren't captured."[3]

DONALD TRUMP IS BEST KNOWN FOR
Real Estate Tycoon
Worth $3.1 billion (estimate by *Forbes*)
Reality TV Star: *The Apprentice*
"You're fired!"
Book: *Art of the Deal*
Trump Tower
Taj Mahal
Birther Movement
Barack Obama was born in Keyna
Crooked Hillary
"Lock 'er up"
Miss USA Pageants

TRUMP PENCE
MAKE AMERICA GREAT AGAIN!
2016

Miss Universe Pageants
Megyn Kelly
Trump University
Mexican Border Wall
Repeal ACA
Rebuild Military
Defends Gun Rights
Vladimir Putin + The Russian Connection
Anti-Transgender
Withdrew from Trans Pacific Partnership
Fired FBI DirectorJames Comey
Married Three Times
First marriage presided over by
Norman Vincent Peale
Supports increased use of Fossil Fuels:
Coal in particular
Says the EPA is a "disgrace"
Says "Global warming is a Chinese hoax"
Never releases income tax returns
Withdrew from Paris climate Agreement

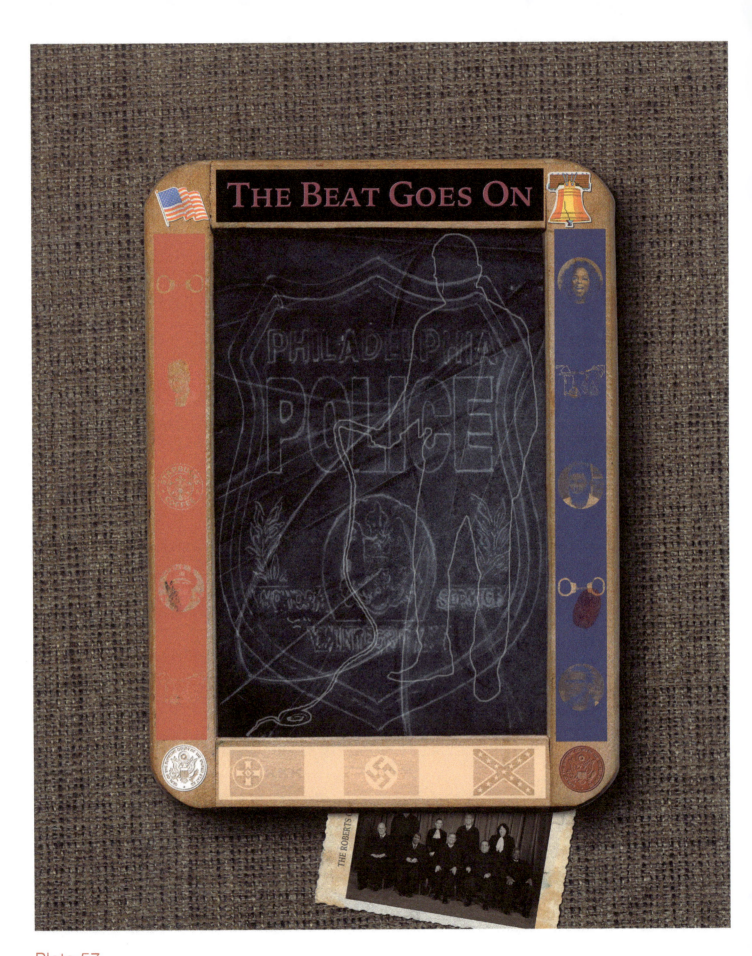

Plate 57
John A. O'Connor, *The Beat Goes On,* 2018. Digital Image, 21 x 17 in.

WHITE LIES MATTER

The incident at a Starbucks in Philadelphia—America's top-rated coffee house chain[1] —happened on April 12, 2018. It focused a nation's attention on the plight of two, seemingly innocent, black men who were arrested for trespassing while they were waiting for a business meeting with a "white local businessman."[2]

Racial profiling in America is nothing new—although it apparently wasn't called that until recently. In fact, racial profiling—under whatever guise it took—is older than America. It was first applied to the "natives" by Spanish King Charles I in 1514 and was even upheld in Maryland murder trials as early as 1642.[3] As early as 1669, the murder of a slave by his master was not only legal, it was sanctioned by the "Casual Slave Killing Act," revised that year in Virginia. And by 1693, Philadelphia (coincidentally?) had "authorized the police to take up any 'Negro' seen 'gradding' about without a pass from his or her master."[4] It made no difference whether the Negro was or was not a slave.

Fast forward to April 14 when Philadelphia Police Commissioner Richard Ross said the policemen who arrested Rashon Nelson and Donte Robinson were disrespected by the two black men. He went on to say that the officers did nothing wrong, and "denied that race had affected the police response."[5]

One week later, the Commissioner, who is also a black man, decided to abruptly change direction. He said, "It is me who in large part made most of the situation worse than it was. So for that, it is my sincere apology to those two men, and even to these officers and to the other

people around this city who I have failed in a variety of ways on this incident." Ross went on to say, "I should have said the officers acted within the scope of the law, and not that they didn't do anything wrong," he said. "Messaging is important, and I failed miserably in this regard."[6]

"Shopping while black," or "Retail Racism" appears to be rampant in 21st century America. It is common knowledge, unfortunately, that many U.S. companies have been sued in the United States for a variety of racial issues and have settled, in some cases for millions of dollars. They include Barneys, Wal-Mart, Southern California Edison, Abercrombie & Fitch, Denny's, BMW, Coca-Cola, CVS, Macy's, Donald Trump, General Electric, Ford Motor Company, Bass Pro Outdoor World LLC and others.

It is a long, long line.

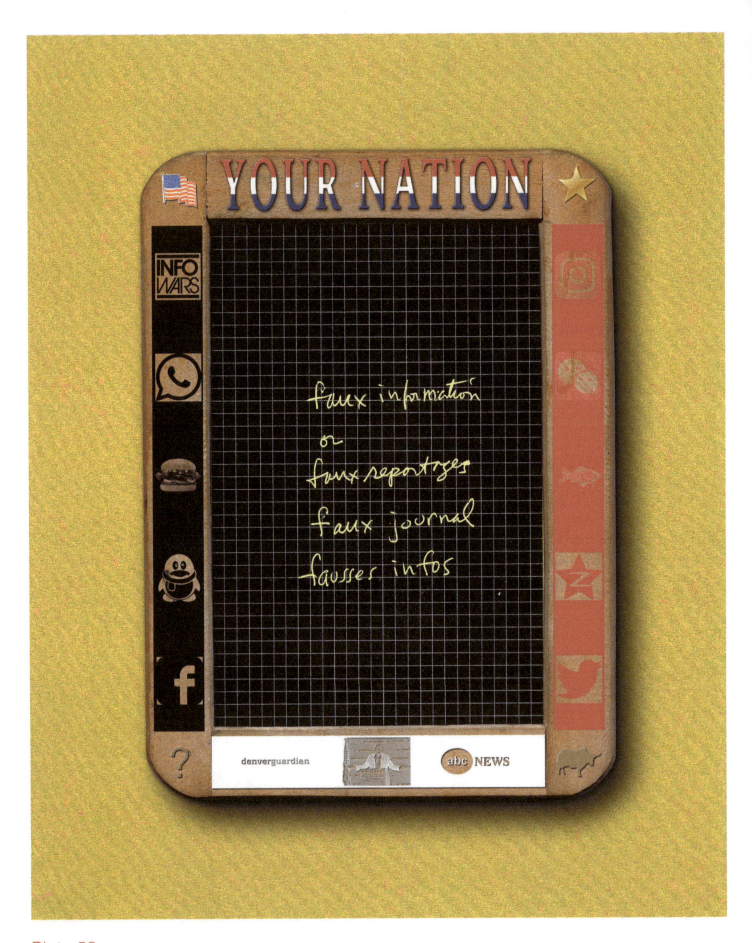

Plate 58

John A. O'Connor, *Your Nation,* 2018. Digital Image, 21 x 17 in.

WHITE LIES MATTER

denverguardian

Yellow journalism has a number of synonyms such as fish story, hype, puffery, tall story, and whopper.[1] Many Americans probably believe that it is a term coined by current U.S. President Donald Trump who repeatedly refers to a great deal of mainstream news reporting as "fake news." But yellow journalism, or fake news, is not new. It has been around for quite awhile, and was a major factor in the U.S. expansion of its overseas empire and into war with Spain in Cuba and the Philippine Islands.[2]

So, where did the term come from? According to many sources, it began in New York (where else?) in the 1890s as Joseph Pulitzer and William Randolph Hearst, two of America's most heralded newspaper publishers, battled it out—mano a mano—in a competition to dominate New York City's journalism market.

But the term itself apparently came from a comic strip called *Hogan's Alley* originally published in the *New York World*—Pulitzer's paper. It featured a character known as the Yellow Kid, and evidently was so popular that it greatly increased sales of Pulitzer's *World*. Not to be outdone, Hearst hired the cartoonist of Hogan's Alley, Richard Outcault, away from the *World*. Pulitzer, in retaliation, hired another cartoonist to continue the comic strip for his paper. The result of the so-called "battle over the Yellow Kid" culminated in the term "yellow journalism."[3]

Yellow journalism then precipitated the U.S. entry into war over Cuba. "The most famous anecdote surrounding Hearst's zeal for the war involves a legendary communication between illustrator Frederick Remington and Hearst. As the story goes, Remington, who had been sent to Cuba to cover the insurrection, cabled to Hearst that there was no war to cover. Hearst allegedly replied with, 'You furnish the pictures. I'll furnish the war.' "[4]

There is also evidence that yellow journalism as "fake news" originated in 1894 in an illustration in *Puck* magazine featuring frenzied "gentlemen" holding newspapers with headings such as "Humbug News," "Cheap Sensation, and, yes, "Fake News."[5] Ironically, *Puck* was eventually purchased by William Randolph Hearst.[6] And, even more ironically, the most prestigious award given to journalists is the Pulitzer Prize first given in 1917[7] —the year before Hearst's *Puck* magazine ceased publication because of lack of interest. It is also quite understandable, that in subsequent years, many Pulitzer Prizes went to none other than *The New York World*.

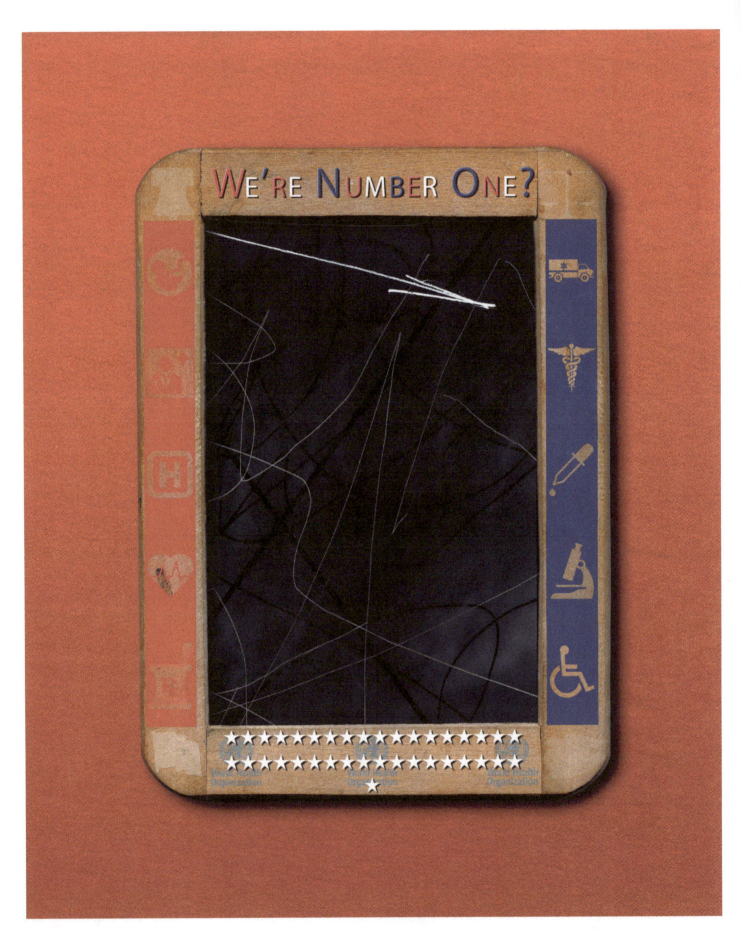

Plate 59

John A. O'Connor, *We're Number One?,* 2018. Digital Image, 21 x 17 in.

WE'RE NUMBER ONE?

Many Americans believe we have the best health care system in the world. Many studies do not support that belief, but *Forbes* disputes that conclusion.[1] Dr. Gary Price and his contributing author, Tim Norbeck, contend that the American Health Care System (Is there really an American Health Care System?) is harder to manage because of the huge U.S. population of 323 million. It states that all of the countries recently cited as having better health care systems are far smaller than the U.S., and therefore they have far fewer problems managing "health care outcomes."[2] It goes on to state that "poverty and other social determinants [in the U.S.] have a significant impact on our health and healthcare costs."[3] It continues, "Ezekiel J. Emanuel, MD, observes that 'administrative costs contribute significantly to the cost difference between the U.S. and others used in the comparison'" and that is a point on which everyone agrees.[4] The authors conclude that American medicine performs significantly more "high-margin, high volume procedures" [like knee replacements] than, for example, the Netherlands.[5] And, finally, American health care costs more because of those damn lawyers who chase ambulances and find unlimited reasons to sue doctors for malpractice. They even say, "No other country has our onerous liability laws."[6]

So, where does the American Health Care System rank in the world? Well, if you accept the *Forbes* article (and its explanations), the U.S. would be number one if only poverty, suicide, murder by guns, car crashes and resultant deaths, obesity and diabetes were not the world's highest, and if drugs were less expensive, housing was improved, jobs were better, and reporting of all health issues were standardized throughout the world. Then, the U.S. might be fairly judged.[7] Then we could convincingly yell, "We're Number One!"

Okay. They're all convincing reasons aren't they? Or, are they? For example, nearly 26 million Americans still don't have any health insurance at all.[8] The World Health Organization ranks the U.S. Health Care System at number 37 in the world—behind Greece (13), Iceland (15), and close ally Saudi Arabia (26). We are, however, ahead of Slovenia and Barbados.[9] Yet, U.S. citizens spent an average of $10,348 per person on healthcare in 2016, while Japanese citizens spent an average of $4,519.[10] Japanese women live an average of six years longer than American women while Japanese men live an average of four years longer than American men.[11]

So, We're Number One?

Plate 60

John A. O'Connor, *Who Knew?,* 2018. Digital Image, 21 x 17 in.

White Lies Matter

FREEDOM OF THE PRESS

The Constitution of the United States of America guarantees that we Americans have access to information that the government can't, doesn't, and won't suppress—the freest press in the world. Right?

If that were only true. Apparently most Americans believed that it was, until the recent spate of fake news hit the airwaves, accompanied by the revival of so-called yellow [print] journalism. But since a lot of Americans believe that we have the best health care in the world, do they also seriously believe that we have true freedom of speech, of expression and of the press? Well, do we?

On the "2018 World Press Freedom Index," the United States ranks number 45.[2] That is behind Romania (44), Burkina Faso (41), Lithuania (36), Namibia (26), Ghana (23), Estonia (12), and even Jamaica (6). Almost all European countries rank ahead of us too! In fact, so do several Central and South American countries.

Of course, this is only one group's opinion. Freedom House says the U.S. has a free press, but it also says, "Press freedom globally has declined to its lowest levels in 13 years, thanks both to new threats to journalists and media outlets in major democracies, and to further crackdowns on independent media in authoritarian countries like Russia and China."[3] It continues, "Borrowing a

Trump has labeled the news media as 'enemies of the people.' "[4] And, even though this organization states that the "United States remains one of the most press-friendly countries in the world," it does note that "recent presidents have sought to limit their exposure to reporters."[5] It even reports that President Obama "pursued a crackdown on federal officials who leaked information to the press, while many journalists chafed at what they regarded as excessive efforts to control access to the Obama White House."[6]

So what can we learn from this? The U.S. Constitution may say that we are guaranteed freedom of speech, of expression, and of the press, but we are currently witnessing a continuing decline of these "freedoms" in the U.S. and around the world.

And, in America, perhaps the most exaggerated visual image of this erosion is represented by kneeling football players. But, not to worry because the National football League recently has institutionalized a program to limit that freedom of expression ("Fire the sons a bitches!") that is supported by many Americans, U.S. corporations, and Donald Trump—the President of the United States. Pardon me, but apparently those constitutional guarantees are really relative. Who knew?

FIEFDOM OF THE PREZ

WHITE LIES MATTER

About John A. O'Connor

John A. O'Connor is a well-known American artist primarily recognized for his *Chalkboard Series,* a group of works that repeatedly question the boundaries between reality and illusion.

Born in Twin Falls, Idaho, in 1940, John grew up in Sacramento, California, where he attended Sacramento City College to study architectural engineering before moving to Mexico City to study art and architecture. In 1960, he returned to California and received his A.B. with Honors in 1961 and his M.A.A. in 1963 in painting and drawing from the University of California–Davis.

He taught art at the University of California–Davis from 1961-63, the University of California–Santa Barbara from 1963-64, Blake College, Valle de Bravo, Mexico from 1964-65, and Ohio University, Athens from 1965-69. Beginning in 1969, he taught art at the University of Florida (UF), Gainesville. He was named Professor of Art in 1985, a position he held until his retirement in 2005.

During his time at the University of Florida, he taught courses in painting, drawing, design, art and engineering, computer art, performance art, art history, art law (with the UF Levin College of Law), and arts policy. He also originated, implemented, and taught in the M.B.A. Degree with Specialization in Arts Administration Program. In 1987-88, he was the Acting Chairman of the Department of Art.

In 1980-82, John A. O'Connor was Director of the Appalachian Center for Crafts, and a Division Director of the Tennessee Arts Commission. In 1983-84 and 1988-89, he served as the Faculty Program Consultant to the Florida Board of Regents. O'Connor also founded, and was the Executive Director of the Florida Higher Education Arts Network (FHEAN) from 1985-2005.

From 1988 through 2005 he was also founder and director of the UF CENTER FOR THE ARTS AND PUBLIC POLICY (CAPP). A sample of programs sponsored or co-sponsored by CAPP includes *Art and Healing; Controversial Public Art, the Legal and Ethical Dimensions; Censorship and Obscenity in the Arts: Public Attitudes/ Legal Problems; Before and After Columbus: The Use and Misuse of the Past; Women in the Nineties: Sex, Power and Politics; and Culture and Art and the Livability of Communities.*

O'Connor has had thirty-six solo exhibitions of his paintings in galleries and museums nationwide including the Ringling Museum, Sarasota, Florida; the Santa Barbara Museum of Art, California; the Pensacola Museum of Art, Florida and the Cornell Fine Arts Museum at Rollins College, Winter Park, Florida. His art has also been exhibited in more than two hundred group shows including the *33rd International Festival of Painting* at the Château Musée (Mediterranean Museum of Contemporary Art), Cagnes-sur-Mer, France (one of sixteen American artists invited), and the *50th Annual All Florida Invitational* at the Boca Raton Museum of Art (one of fourteen Florida artists invited).

John has received numerous awards including a *Southern Arts Federation/National Endowment for the Arts Fellowship* in 1992-93, a State of Florida *Individual Artist's Fellowship* in 1991-92, and in 2002-03, a University of Florida *Professorial Excellence Program Award.*

WHITE LIES MATTER

His paintings and drawings are in numerous public and private collections in the U.S. and abroad including the State of California Collection, the Ringling Museum of Art, the Cornell Fine Arts Museum, Bechtel Corporation, Alabama Power and Light, Cole National Corporation and IBM Corporation.

Although John is primarily known for his paintings, most people are unaware that nearly all of his art works since 2005 have been computer generated and digitally produced. John is no newcomer to technology and art. In the 1950s, when he studied architectural engineering, he also minored in mathematics and foreign language. In the 1960s, as an art instructor at Ohio University, he introduced faculty and students to both audio art and performance art. In 1970, he teamed up with a Professor of Aerospace and Engineering Science and Mechanics at the University of Florida, to introduce art and engineering students to a unique course titled "Creativity, Innovation, and Design." This course united art, engineering, and technology concerns and led, by 1974, to the UF Department of Art awarding its first M.F.A. degree with an emphasis in Computer Art—a program with which John collaborated.

In 1976, John also introduced "Performance as Art" to UF's art curriculum, the first performance art course taught for credit in an U.S. college or university. At the same time, he introduced video art to the Department of Art curriculum, and produced his first interactive video art-performance piece titled *Red Tape Stations of the Cross* exploring the corruption and waste associated with government bureaucracy.

NOTES

Plate 1
White Lies Matter: **Decoding American Deceptionalism**

1. Maria L. Cronley, Frank R. Kardes, and Scott A. Hawkins, "Influences on the Illusory Truth Effect in Consumer Judgment," *Association for Consumer Research,* 2006. Accessed at *acrwebsite.org.*
2. Ralph Hertwig, Gerd Gigerenzer, and Ulrich Hoffrage, "The Reiteration Effect in Hindsight Bias," *Psychological Review,* 1997, Vol. 104, No. 1, 194-202. Accessed at *library.mpib.berlin.mpg.de.*

Plate 2
Columbus Discovered America, Right?

1. "Columbus Day Poem." Accessed December 10, 2017 at *scholastic.com.*
2. "History of the Caribbean (West Indies)," *History World.* Accessed November 28, 2017 at *historyworld.net.*
3. Ibid., 3.
4. Page 22 of Southey, T. (1827). *Chronological history of the West Indies (vol. 1).* London: Longman, Rees, Orme, Brown, and Green. Accessed February 20, 2018, at *understandingprejudice.org.*
5. "Leif Eriksson," *History.* Accessed November 28, 2017 at *history.com.*
6. Gareth Cook, "Did the Solutreans settle America first?," *Boston Globe,* March 18, 2012. Accessed at *bostonglobe.com.*
7. "Columbus Day," History. Accessed February 21, 2018 at history.com.
8. Bryan Strong, "Slavery and Colonialism Make Up the True Legacy of Columbus," *New York Times,* November 4, 1989. Accessed at *nytimes.com.*

Plate 3
The First Thanksgiving

1. James W. Loewen, "The Truth about The First Thanksgiving," November 29, 2002, *Trinicenter.com.* Accessed at *trinicenter.com.*
2. "Christopher Columbus," *History.* Accessed November 28, 2017 at *history.com.*
3. Ibid.
4. Loewen, "The Truth about The First Thanksgiving."
5. Russ Kick, "The Virginia Colonists at Jamestown Practiced Cannibalism," *disinfo,* February 25, 2010. Accessed at *disinfo.com.*
6. Paula Neely, "Jamestown Colonists Resorted to Cannibalism," May 3, 2015, *National Geographic.* Accessed at *news.nationalgeographic.com.*

If material that was sourced online contains a publication date, the accessed date is not included.

Plate 4
Onward Christian Founders

1. Jeff Schweitzeer, "Founding Fathers: We Are Not a Christian Nation," April 28, 2015, *HuffPost.* Accessed at *huffingtonpost.com.*
2. Ibid.
3. Ibid.
4. Ibid.
5. Ibid.
6. Ibid.
7. Richard Albert, *Constitutional Dismemberment* (Boston: Boston College Law School Research Paper No. 424 Draft, 2016), 26.

Plate 5
By George

1. "Cherry Tree Myth," *George Washington's Mount Vernon.* Accessed December 4, 2017 at *mountvernon.org.*
2. Ibid.
3. Ibid.
4. Ibid.
5. Ibid.
6. *The Joice Heth Exhibit, The Lost Museum Archive.* Accessed December 4, 2017 at *lostmuseum.cuny.edu.*
7. "Conotocarious," George Washington's Mount Vernon. Accessed October 29, 2018 at *mountvernon.org.*

Plate 6
Measuring Value

1. Guy Reel, "American Values," *Common Dreams,* April 20, 2005. Accessed at *commondreams.org.*

Plate 7
The Golden Rule

Morning News, Sec.2, 9, May 3, 1965. Accessed at *quoteinvestigator.com.*
2. Stephen Anderson, "The Golden Rule: Not So Golden Anymore," *Philosophy Now.* Accessed November 26, 2017 at *philosophynoworg..*
3. Michael Teague, "Five Philosophers on Money and Wealth," *equities.com,* December 24, 2013. Accessed at *equities.com.*
4. Ibid.
5. Ibid.

Plate 8
A Certain "T"

1. David Corn, "Watch Donald Trump Lecture Americans for Not Paying Taxes, *Mother Jones,* October 2, 2016. Accessed at *motherjones.com.*
2. Albert Henry Smyth, *The Writings of Benjamin Franklin,* Vol. X (1789-1790), (New York: MacMillian, 1907), 69.
3. Fred Shapiro, "Quotes Uncovered: Death and Taxes," *Freakonomics,* February 17, 2011. (From his book, *The Yale Book of Quotations.*) Accessed at *freakonomics.com.*
4. *The New Dictionary of Cultural Literacy, Third Edtion,* (New York: Houghton Mifflin Company, 2005), *Dictionary.com.* Accessed November 26, 2017 at *dictionary.com.*
5. "1 Timothy 6:7," *The Holy Bible, New International Version,* (Grand Rapids, Michigan: Zondervan, 2011).

Plate 9
USAUSAUSA

1. From Francis Scott Key obituary, *Baltimore American,* January 13, 1843 in "Reading 2: Francis Scott Key and the Writing of The Star-Spangled Banner." Accessed December 9, 2017 at *nps.gov.*
2. Francis Scott Key, "Defense of Fort M'Henry," (Baltimore, Maryland, 1814). Retrieved from the Library of Congress. Accessed December 11, 2017 at *loc.gov.*
3. "World Prison Populations." *BBC News.* Accessed December 9, 2017 at *news.bbc.co.uk.*
4. "Getting Vietnam War Into Classrooms is Still a Battle," *Los Angeles Times,* May 1, 1995. Accessed at *articles.latimes.com.* (Although textbooks in 2017 are including more material on the Vietnam War, numerous educators have told me that it is still controversial to do

Plate 10
The Other Supremes
1. Bernard Schwartz, *A Book of Legal Lists: The Best and Worst in American Law* (New York: Oxford University Press, 1997), 70. Accessed at *books.google.com.*
2. Fred Bronson, *The Billboard Book of Number 1 Hits,* (New York: Billboard Books, 2003), 265. Accessed at *google.books.com.*
3. "Dred Scott Case," *History.com.* Accessed December 9, 2017 at *history.com.*
4. Andrew Shankman, ed., *The World of the Revolutionary American Republic: Land, Labor, and the Conflict for a Continent,* (New York: Routledge, 2014), 361. Accessed at *books.google.com.*

Plate 11
Women's Suffrage

1. Robert Cooney, "Taking a New Look—The Enduring Significance of the American Woman Suffrage Movement," *MITH Maryland Institute for Technology in the Humanities,* University of Maryland. Accessed December 4, 2017 at *mith.umd.edu.*
2. "19th Amendment," *History.* Accessed December 9, 2017 at *history.com.*
3. Ibid.
4. Newport, Frank, "Wyoming, North Dakota and Mississippi Most Conservative," *GALLUP News,* January 31, 2017. Accessed at *news.gallup.com.*
5. Kerry Drake, "Estelle Reel, First Woman Elected to Statewide Office in Wyoming, *WyoHistory.org.* Accessed December 9, 2017 at *wyohistory.org.*
6. "Milestones for Women in American Politics," *CAWP Center for American Women and Politics,* Eagleton Institute of Politics, Rutgers University. Accessed December 9, 2017 at *cawp.rutgers.edu.*

Plate 12
White Knights?

1. "Ku Klux Klan," *Southern Poverty Law Center.* Accessed December 10, 2017 at *splcenter.org.*
2. Chester L. Quarles, *The Ku Klux Klan and Related American Racialist and Antisemitic Organizations,* (Jefferson, North Carolina and London: McFarland & Company, Inc., 1999), 8. Accessed at *books.google.com.*
3. "Active Hate Groups 2016," *Southern Poverty Law Center*, February 15, 2017. Accessed at *splcenter.org.*
4. Maureen Dowd, "Trump, Neo-Nazis and the Klan," *The New York Times*, August 19, 2017. Accessed at *nytimes.com.*
5. "Grant, Reconstruction, and the KKK," *PBS.* Accessed December 10, 2017 at *pbs.org.*
6. Andrew Glass, "Ku Klux Klan founded Dec. 24, 1865," *Politico,* December 24, 2007. Accessed at *politico.com.*
7. Arthur Conan Doyle, "The Five Orange Pips," in the *Arthur Conan Doyle Encyclopedia.* Accessed at *arthur-conan-doyle.com.*
8. David Cunningham, "Top 5 Questions About the KKK," *PBS.* Accessed December 10, 2017 at *pbs.org.*
9. Quarles, *The Ku Klux Klan,* 8.

Plate 13
Redacted

1. Louis Edward Inglehart, ed., *Press and Speech Freedoms in the World, from Antiquity Until 1998: A Chronology,* (Portsmouth, New Hampshire: Greenwood Publishing Group), 171. Accessed at *books.google.com.*
2. Robert Cashill "Way Out West: Classic Lines from Hollywood's Dirty Blonde," *Biography,* August 15, 2017. Accessed at *biography.com.*
3. Rochelle Gurstein, *The Repeal of Reticence: America's Cultural and Legal Struggles Over Free Speech, Obscenity, Sexual Liberation, and Modern Art* (New York: Farrar, Straus and Giroux, 2016), 127. Accessed at *books.google. com.*
4. Louise A. Merriam, "Anthony Comstock, the YMCA, and the New York Society for the Suppression of Vice," January 24, 2018, *Continuum* (University of Minnesota Libraries.) Accessed on October 30, 2018 at *continuum.umn.edu.*

Plate 14
Whiskeygate

1. Iain Topliss, *The Comic Worlds of Peter Arno, William Steig, Charles Addams and Saul Steinberg,* (Baltimore and London: Johns Hopkins University Press, 2005), 241.
2. Timothy Rives, "Grant, Babcock, and the Whiskey Ring," *Prologue Magazine* [National Archives], Fall 2000, vol. 32, No. 3. Accessed on April 2, 2018 at *archives.gov.*
3. "1870 dollars in 2016." Accessed on April 2, 2018 at *in2013dollars.com.*
4. Rives, Op. Cit.
5. Ibid.
6. "Joseph Pulitzer in History of American Journalism," *Shmoop.* Accessed April 3, 2018 at *shmoop.com.*
7. Rives, Op cit.
8. Mark H. Waymack and James F. Harris, *The Book of Classic American Whiskeys,* (Chicago and La Salle, Illinois: Open Court Publishing company, 1995),35. Accessed at *books.google.com.*
9. Rives, Op Cit.
10. Ibid

Plate 15
A Big Stick

1. McCullough, David, *The Path Between the Seas: The Creation of the Panama Canal, 1870–1914,* New York: Simon & Schuster, 1977, 224.
2. "American Canal Construction." Accessed March 20, 2018 at Autoridad del Canal de Panama.
3. "The 1903 Treaty and Qualified Independence." Accessed March 21, 2018 at *country studies.us.* (Source: U.S. Library of Congress)
4. Ibid.
5. "American Canal Construction." Op. cit.
6. Ibid.

Plate 16
Normalcy

1. "Teapot Dome Scandal," *History.* Accessed on March 21, 2018 at history.com.
2. Ibid.
3. Ibid
4. "The Roaring Twenties," *History.* Accessed on March 21, 2018 at history.com..
5. Ibid.
6. Ibid.
7. Ibid.
8. Ibid.
9. Thomas Streissguth, *The Roaring Twenties,* Revised Edition (New York: Facts on File, 2007), 84.
10. John Jay Greer, ed., *Public Opinion and Polling Around the World: A Historical Encyclopedia* (Santa Barbara, CA: ABC CLIO, 2004), 100.

Plate 17
That Old Black Magic

1. "*Billboard Top 100,* 1943." Accessed December 9, 2107 at *billboardtop100of.com.*
2. "Definition of Black magic," *Merriam-Webster.* Accessed December 1, 2017 at *merriam-webster.com.*
3. "Seven ways oil and gas drilling is bad news for the environment," *The Wilderness Society.* Accessed December 1, 2017 at *wilderness.org.*
4. Ibid.

WHITE LIES MATTER

Plate 18
Third Time's a Charm

1. "1940: FDR's Third Presidential Campaign," *See How They Ran!* Accessed December 10, 2017 at *roosevelthouse.hunter.cuny.edu.*
2. Ibid.
3. "Franklin D. Roosevelt Campaign Address at Boston, Massachusetts," October 30, 1940. *The American Presidency Project.* Accessed at *presidency.ucsb.edu.*
4. "WWII Facts & Figures," *World War II Foundation.* Accessed on December 10, 2017 at *wwiifoundation.org.*

Plate 19
Hypocritic Oath

1. DeNeen L. Brown, " 'You've got bad blood': The horror of the Tuskegee syphilis experiment," *The Washington Post,* May 16, 2017. Accessed at *The Washington Post (WP Company LLC).*
2. James H. Jones, *Bad Blood: The Tuskegee Syphilis Experiment* (New York: The Free Press, 1981, 1993), 1. Accessed at *amazon.com.*
3. Ibid., 5.
4. Sarah Kaplan, "Dr. Irwin Schatz, the first lonely voice against infamous Tuskegee study, dies at 83," *The Washington Post,* April 20, 2015. Accessed at *The Washington Post (WP Company LLC).*
5. "The Tuskegee Syphilis Study." Accessed December 9, 2017 at *history.ucsb.edu.*
6. Ibid.
7. "Fact Sheet on the 1946-1948 U.S. Public Health Service Sexually Transmitted Diseases (STD) Inoculation Study," *U.S. Department of Health & Human Services.* Accessed December 10, 2017 at *hhs.gov.*
8. Ibid.

Plate 20
Interment or Internment

1. "Transcript of Executive Order 9066: Resulting in the Relocation of Japanese (1942)," *www.ourdocuments.gov.* Accessed December 23, 2017 at *ourdocuments.gov.*
2. Lawrence Walker, "February 19, 1942 Japanese American Internment," *Pure History.* Accessed at *purehistory.org.*
3. Paul Moke, *Earl Warren and the Struggle for Justice* (Lanham, Maryland: Lexington Books, 2015), 35. Accessed at *books.google.com.*
4. White, G. Edward, "The Unacknowledged Lesson: Earl Warren and the Japanese Relocation Controversy." *VQR,* Autumn 1979, Volume 55, no. 4, published December 12, 2003. Accessed at *vqr.org.*
5. "Facts and Case Summary—Korematsu v. U.S.," *United States Courts.* Accessed on December 9, 2017 at *uscourts.gov.*
6. Ibid.
7. Ibid.

Plate 21
NASA"s Nazis

1. Wendy Lower, book review of *Operation Paperclip,* by Annie Jacobsen, February 28, 2014, *The New York Times.* Accessed at *nytimes.com.*
2. "Operation Paperclip Casefile," dossier compiled by Agent Orange, August 8, 1997. Accessed at *conspiracyacrhive.com.*
3. Ibid.
4. Ibid.
5. Ibid.

Plate 22
Alienation

1. "1947 Roswell UFO Incident," *The International UFO Museum Research Center.* Accessed on December 23, 2017 at *roswellufomuseum.com.*
2. Ibid.
3. Matt Blitz, "The Real Story Behind the Myth of Area 51," *PM,* September 14, 2017. Accessed at *popularmechanics.com.*
4. Stephen Regenold, "Lonesome Highway to Another World," *The New York Times,* April 13, 2007. Accessed at *nytimes.com.*
5. Evans Andrews, "U.S. Air Force Closes the Book on UFOs, 45 Years Ago," *History,* December 17, 2014. Accessed at *history.com.*

WHITE LIES MATTER

Plate 23
Charming Billy

1. Billy Graham, "The Modesto Manifesto," *Billy Graman Evangelistic Association,* October 24, 2016. Accessed at *billygraham.org.*
2. "10 reasons why Mike Pence's 'Billy Graham Rule' harms us," *Premier Christianity,* April 2, 2017. Accessed at *premierchristianity.com.*
3. David Firestone, "Billy Graham Responds to Lingering Anger Over 1972 Remarks on Jews," *The New York Times,* March 12, 2002. Accessed at *nytimes.com.*
4. Billy Graham, interview by David Frost, "Doubt and Certainties," *BBC Two,* 1964. Accessed at *books.google.com.*
5. "Resolution On Ordination And The Role Of Women In Ministry Southern Baptist Convention," *Southern Baptist Convention,* 1984. Accessed November 27, 2017 at *sbc.net.*
6. David Frost and Billy Graham, *Billy Graham: Personal thoughts of a Public Man,* 1997, 72-74. Accessed November 27, 2017 in *"Billy Graham on Evolution," Letters to Creationists* at *letterstocreationists.wordpress.com.*
7. "Christians Don't Have to Belong to GOP, Democrat Graham Says," *Los Angeles Times,* July 23, 1988. Accessed at *articles.latimes.com.*
8. Kevin M. Cruse, "Billy Graham, 'America's pastor'?, "*The Washington Post.* Accessed June 7, 2018 at *The Washington Post (WP Company LLC)*
9. Achim Nkosi Maseko, *Church Schism & Corruption* (Morrisville, North Carolina: Lulu, 2009), 399. Accessed at *books.google.com.*

Plate 24
The Original Pledge

1. "The Pledge of Alllegiance," (1892 original version), *US history.org.* Accessed December 4, 2017 at *ushistory.org.*
2. Ibid.

Plate 25
You Too?

1. "U-2 Overflights and the Capture of Francis Gary Powers, 1960," in "Milestones: 1953-1960," *Office of the Historian.* Accessed December 10, 2017 at *history.state.gov.*
2. "U-2 Spy Incident," *History.* Accessed December 9, 2017 at *history.com.*
3. Ibid.
4. "U-2 Overflights."
5. "U-2 Spy Incident."
6. Ibid.

Plate 26
Revolution Illusion

1. "The Bay of Pigs Invasion and its Aftermath, April 1961-October 1962," *Office of the Historian.* Accessed December 10, 2017 at *history.state.gov.*
2. Benjamin Ginsberg, *The American Lie: Government by the People and Other Political Fables,* (Boulder, Colorado: Paradigm Publishers, 2007), 3. Accessed December 21, 2017 at *books.google.com.*
3. "Bay of Pigs" 40 Years After," *The National Security Archive.* Accessed December 21, 2017 at *nsarchive2.gwu.edu.*
4. John T. Correll, "Airpower at the Bay of Pigs," *Air Force Magazine,* July 2017. Accessed at *airforcemag.com.*
5. "The Bay of Pigs," *John F. Kennedy Presidential Library and Museum.* Accessed December 5, 2017 at *jfklibrary.org.*

Plate 27
Profiles Encouraged

1. This is my accurately paraphrased version of the document that President John F. Kennedy read from when awarding the "Outstanding Record Citation" to Harry J. Anslinger on September 27, 1962. It was transcribed from the audio version at the Kennedy Presidential Library.
2. David McDonald, "The Racist Roots of Marijuana Prohibition," April 11, 2017, *Foundation for Economic Education.* Accessed at *fee.org.*
3. Russ Belville, "11 US Presidents Who Smoked Marijuana," *High Times,* February 17, 2014. Accessed at *hightimes.com.*
4. Ibid.

Plate 28
Assassin Nation

1. Kuang Kuek Ser, "Map: Here are countries with the world's highest murder rates," *PRI's The World,* June 27, 2016. Accessed at *pri.org.*
2. "U.S. Presidential assassinations and attempts," January 22, 2012, *Los Angeles Times.* Accessed at *timelines.latimes.com.*
3. Ibid.
4. Stephanie Schoppert, "Ten Political Leaders Who Survived Multiple Assassination Attempts," *History Collection.* Accessed December 9, 2017 at *historycollection.co.*
5. Eli Watkins, "Will Trump allow release of final JFK assassination documents?," October 6, 2017. *CNN.* Accessed at *cnn.com.*

Plate 29
Grandma's Nightshirt

1.Paul Aron, *Mysteries in History: From Prehistory to the Present* (Santa Barbara, California: ABC-CLIO, Inc., 2006), 396. Accessed at *books.google.com.*
2. Ben Westcott, "Afghanistan: 16 years, thousands dead and no clear end in sight," *CNN,* October 31, 2017. Accessed at *cnn.com.*
3. "Vietnam War Facts," *HistoryNet.* Accessed December 7, 2017 at *historynet.com.*
4. Ibid.
5. Lieutenant Commander Pat Patterson, U.S. Navy, "The Truth About Tonkin," *Naval History Magazine,* February 2008, Vol. 22, No. 1., *U.S. Naval Institute.* Accessed at *usni.org.*
6. Ibid
7. Jesse Greenspan, "The Gulf of Tonkin Incident, 50 Years Ago," *HISTORY,* August 1, 2004. Accessed at *history.com.*
8. Patterson, "The Truth About Tonkin."
9. Mark Murrmann, "50 Years Ago Today: Congress Authorizes Vietnam War Under Bullshit Pretense," *Mother Jones,* August 7, 2014. Accessed at *motherjones.com.*

Plate 30
Winning Hearts and Minds

1. "Glossary of Military Terms and Slang," *Military.com.* Accessed December 6, 2017 at *military.com.*
2. Douglas Lindner, "The My Lai Massacre Trial," *JURIST,* March 2000. Accessed at *jurist.org.*
3. "Calley charged for My Lai massacre," *History.* Accessed December 6, 2017 at *history.com.*
4. Lindner, "The My Lai Massacre Trial."
5. "Colin Powell," *HISTORY.* Accessed December 6, 2017 at *history.com.*
6. Charles Mohr, "Carter Credibility Issue: Calley and Vietnam War," *The New York Times,* May 21, 1976. Accessed at *nytimes.com.*
7. "Calley charged for My Lai massacre," *History.*
8. "The Vietnam Question," *PBS.* Accessed December 6, 2017 at *pbs.org.*
9. Lyndon B. Johnson, "Remarks at a Dinner Meeting of the Texas Electric Cooperatives, Inc.," *The American Presidency Project,* May 4, 1965. Accessed at *presidency.ucsb.edu.*
10. Philippians 4:7, *The Holy Bible, New International Version,* (Grand Rapids, Michigan: Zondervan, 2011)
11. Lindner, "The My Lai Massacre Trial."

Plate 31
Four Dead in Ohio

1. "Kent State Incident," *History.* Accessed December 3, 2017 at *history.com.*
2. John Kifner, "8 Hurt as Shooting Follows Reported Sniping at Rally," *The New York Times,* May 5, 1970. Accessed at *nytimes.com.*
3. J. Gregory Payne, "Appendices," ("Governor Rhodes' Speech at Press Conference," Kent, Ohio, May 3, 1970, Kent Fire House), *MAY 4 Archive.org.* Accessed at *may4archive.org.*
4. "Kent State Shootings," *Ohio History Central.* Accessed December 3, 2017 at *ohiohistorycentral.org.*

Plate 32
Tricky Dick
1. Select Committee on Presidential Campaign Activities" (The Watergate Committee), June 27, 1974, *United States Senate.* Accessed at *U.S. Senate.*
2. Ibid.
3. "Watergate Fast Facts," *CNN* (updated June 10, 2017). Accessed at *cnn.com.*
4. Carol Kilpatrick, "Nixon Tells Editors, 'I'm Not a Crook,' " *The Washington Post,* November 18, 1973, A01. Accessed at *washingtonpost.com.*
5. "Douglas, Helen Gahagan," History, Art & Archives, United States House of Representatives. Accessed on November 2, 2018 at history.house.gov.

Plate 33
Co-incidents
1. Theodore H. Moran, *Multinational Corporations and the Politics of Dependence: Copper in Chile* (Princeton, New Jersey: Princeton University Press, 1974), 6.
2. "CIA Reveals Covert Acts in Chile," *CBS News,* September 11, 2000. Accessed at *cbsnews.com.*
3. Ibid.
4. William R. Keech, "Democracy, Dictatorship and Economic Performance in Chile" (paper presented at the Latin American Meeting of the Econometric Society, Santiago Chile, July 28-30, 2004.) Accessed at *fmww.bc.edu.*
5. "Salvador Allende," *Biography.* Accessed December 9, 2017 at *biography.com.*

White Lies Matter

Plate 34
Just Plain Jimmy

1. Jason Maaoz, "Jimmy Carter's Jewish Problem," *Jewish Press.com*, November 22, 2006. Accessed at *jewishpress.com*.
2. Jen Hayden, "Is the White House so fragile that it won't stand for a Democrat being celebrated?" *Alternet*, May 2, 2017. Accessed at *alternet.org*.
3. "Trump vetoes Carter Tribute," *Buenos Aires Herald.com*, April 28, 2017. Accessed at *buenosairesherald.com*.
4. robla, "What Donald Trump and Jimmy Carter have in common," *Daily Kos*, January 16, 2016. Accessed at *Kos Media LLC*. [robla is pen name of Robert Lanphier]
5. "Jimmy Carter Leaves Southern Baptists," *ABC News*, October 20, 2000. Accessed at *abcnews.go.com*.

Plate 35
In Sight

1. "Address to the Nation on the Iran Arms and Contra Aid Controversy," March 4, 1987. Accessed at *reaganlibrary.archives.gov*.
2. Edited by Malcolm Byrne, "The Iran-Contra Affair 30 Years Later: A Milestone in Post-Truth Politics," *National Security Archive*, November 25, 2016. Accessed at *nsarchive2.gwu.edu*.
3. Ronald Reagan, "Remarks at the Annual Dinner of the Conservative Political Action Conference." *The American Presidency Project*, March 1, 1985. Accessed at *presidency.ucsb.edu*.
4. Joel Brinkley, "Arms to Iran Weren't for Hostages, Reagan Says," *The New York Times*, December 4, 1987. Accessed at *nytimes.com*.

Plate 36
Saint Ronald

1. R. K. Ayers, *Misused: Revealing the Fact. Fiction, and Truth of Biblical Encouragement,* (Bloomington, Indiana: WestBow Press, 2016),1. Accessed December 23, 2017 at *books.google.com*.
Ayers does not identify where or when Reagan said this. *IZQuotes* states Reagan delivered those words at his Address to the annual meeting of the Phoenix Chamber of Commerce on March 30, 1961. I have read and re-read that document and cannot find Reagan's "quote" anywhere in the address. In addition, on April 6, 2015, *Ring of Fire Radio, MPN News*, stated that, "TX Public School Posts Made Up Quotes from Reagan, Bible, George Washington To Promote Christianity." [Accessed at *mintpressnews.com*.] Carey Wedler, in "Texas Schools Caught Manipulating Quotes to Push Christianity on Students," *Global Research,* August 8, 2015, says, "The Freedom from Religion Foundation, a non-profit organization, says these quotes are false. It recently wrote a letter to the school district asking that they correct their misattributions. Staff Attorney Sam Grover called the alleged Reagan quote 'dubious, and, incidentally, intellectually lazy since that is not a direct quotation.' "
2. Susan J. Douglas, "The Enduring Lies of Ronald Reagan," *Third World Traveler,* June 19, 2007. Accessed at *thirdworldtraveler.com*.
3. Ibid.
4. Paul Kengor and Patricia Clark Doerner, "Reagan's Darkest Hour, *National Review,* January 22, 2008. Accessed at *nationalreview.com*.
5. Adam Winkler, "The Secret History of Guns," *The Atlantic,* September 2011. Accessed at *theatlantic.com*.
6. Arica L. Coleman, "When the NRA Supported Gun Control," *Time,* July 29, 2016 (correction appended July 31). Accessed at *time.com*.
7. Julia Manchester, "Ronald Reagan named to Labor Department hall of fame," *The Hill,* August 24, 2017. Accessed at *thehill.com*.
8. Joe Davidson, "Induction of union-busting Reagan into Labor's Hall of Honor shocks union," *The Washington Post,* September 19, 2017. Accessed at *The Washington Post (WP Company LLC)*.

Plate 37
Magog Be With You

1. George H.W. Bush, "Read my lips: no new taxes," *Time*. Accessed December 10, 2017 at *content.time.com*.
2. "Nightly News," *NBC News,* June 12, 2012. Accessed December 10, 2017 from Closed Captioning that was broadcast along with this program at *nbcnews.com*.
3. "Points of Light." Accessed at *pointsoflight.org*.
4. Greg Grandin, "How the Iraq War Began in Panama, *TomDispatch,* December 21, 2014. Accessed at *tomdispatch.com*.
5. Alexandria Robbins, "George W., Knight of Eulogia," *The Atlantic,* May 2000. Accessed at *theatlantic.com*.
6. Holland, Joshua, "The First Iraq War Was Also Sold to the Public Based on a Pack of Lies, *Moyers & Company,* June 27, 2014. Accessed at *billmoyers.com*.
7. "President George H. W. Bush's Address on Iraq's Invasion of Kuwait, 1990," *Council on Foreign Relations,* August 8. 1990. Accessed at *cfr.org*.

Plate 38
Slick Willie

1. Matthew Hoffman, "The Bill Clinton we knew at Oxford: Apart from smoking dope (and not inhaling), what else did he learn over here? College friends share their memories with Matthew Hoffman," *Independent,* October 10, 1992. Accessed at *independent.co.uk.*
2. Luke Crafton, "Must Read: Bill Clinton's 1968 Letter Home from Oxford," *Antiques Roadshow, PBS*, April 6, 2015, updated October 18, 2016. Accessed at *pbs.org.*
3. Hoffman, "The Bill Clinton.".
4. Olivia B. Waxman, "Bill Clinton Said He 'Didn't Inhale' 25 Years Ago—But the History of U.S. Presidents and Drugs Is Much Older," March 29, 2017, *Time.* Accessed at *time.com.*
5. Ibid.

Plate 39
The Oval Orifice

1. Lily Rothman, "The Story Behind Bill Clinton's Infamous Denial," *Time,* January 26, 2015. Accessed at *time.com.*
2. Melinda Henneberger, "The President Under Fire on the Right; Conservative Talk Radio Finding Cause for Revelry," *The New York Times,* January 29, 1998. Accessed at *nytimes.com.*
3. James Barron with Phoebe Hoban, "Public Lives Dueling Soaps," *The New York Times,* January 28, 1998. Accessed at *nytimes.com.*
4. Eric Bradner, "Bill Clinton's alleged sexual misconduct: Who you need to know," *CNN politics,* October 9, 2106. Accessed at *cnn.com.*
5. Ibid.
6. "Bill Clinton Was Expelled from Oxford Over a Rape Incident? *Snopes.* Accessed December 3, 2017 at *snopes.com*
7. Roger Stone and Robert Morrow, "The Secret Abuse Victims of Bill Clinton," *Breitbart,* November 23, 2015. Accessed at *breitbart.com.*

Plate 40
To Know Avail

1. Hillary Clinton on *NPR's Weekend Edition,* January 13, 1996. Accessed at *youtube.com.*
2. Edward McClelland, "Hillary Clinton and Chicago Politics," July 11, 2013, *Chicago 5.* Accessed December 4, 2017 at *nbcchicago.com.*
3. Ibid.
4. Ibid.
5. Bill Dedman, "How the Clintons wrapped up Hillary's thesis," *NBC News.com,* September 6, 2007. Accessed at *nbcnews.com.*
6. Alida Black, "Blazing a Trail: Hillary Clinton, Advocate for Children and the Indigent," *HuffPost,* September 21, 2014.

Accessed at *huffingtonpost.com.*
7. Eliza Relman, "Hillary Clinton decided to go to Yale law school after a Harvard professor told her: 'We don't need any more women at Harvard'," *Business Insider,* September 19, 2017. Accessed at *businessinsider.com.*
8. Peter Overby, "The Clintons Wrote The Book On How Politicians Climb Out Of Middle Class," *NPR,* August 17, 2016. Accessed at *National Public Radio, Inc.*

Plate 41
Smokin' Hot

1. "10 Big Fat Lies and the Liars Who Told Them," June 27, 2014, *Moyers & Company.* Accessed at *billmoyers.com.*
2. "History of Tobacco" *Boston University Medical Center.* Accessed December 10, 2017 at *academic.udayton.edu.*
3. Ibid
4. Ibid
5. Ibid
6. Ibid
7. Ibid
8. Kathleen Michon, "Here's the current status of tobacco lawsuits against cigarette manufacturers," *NOLO.* Accessed December 10, 2017 at *nolo.com.*

Plate 42
Falls Alarm

1. Colin Powell, *It Worked for Me,* (New York: HarperCollins, 2012), 2. Accessed December 10, 2017 at *books. google.com.*
2. Sophie Arie, Ewen MacAskill and David Pallister. "Crude Niger forgeries surface in Italian paper" *theguardian,* July 17, 2003. Accessed at *theguardian.com.*
3. Jonathan Stein and Tim Dickinson, "Lie by Lie: A Timeline of How We Got Into Iraq," *Mother Jones,* September/October 2006. Accessed at *motherjones.com.*
4. Ibid.
5. Michelle, "Since 1776, America has been at war 222 out of 239 years," *Motley News,* March 2, 2015. Accessed at *motleynews.net.*
6. Chris Hedges, *'What Every Person Should Know About War,'* *The New York Times,* July 6, 2003. Accessed at *nytimes.com.*

Plate 43
The Crusade

1. Jackson Lears, "How a War Became a Crusade," *The New York Times,* March 11, 2003. Accessed at *nytimes. com.*
2. Ibid.

WHITE LIES MATTER

Plate 44
Gitmo

1. Donald J. Trump @realDonaldTrump, March 7, 2017. Accessed at *miamiherald.com.*
2. Carol Rosenberg, "Trump blames wrong president for most Guantánamo 'back to battlefield' releases, *Miami Herald,* March 7, 2017. Accessed at *miamiherald.com.*
3. Leopold, Jason, "Obama and Bush: How do the Presidents Compare on Guantánamo Bay?," *Vice,* November 10, 2104. Accessed at *vice.com.*
4. Accessed November 27, 2017 at *navymwrguantanamobay.com.*
5. "O'Kelly's Irish Pub," *NavyMWR Guantanamo Bay.* Accessed November 27, 2017 at *navymwrguantanamobay.com.*
6. "Naval Station Guantanamo Bay, Cuba," *Military INSTALLATIONS.* Accessed December 10, 2017 at *militaryinstallations.dod.mil.*
7."By the numbers," *Miami Herald,* October 25, 2016 (Updated November 8, 2017).Accessed at *miamiherald.com.*
8. Molly Crabapple, "It Don 't Gitmo Better Than This," *Vice,* July 31, 2013. Accessed at *vice.com.*

Plate 45
Poetic Justice

1. "Poetic justice," *Oxford Reference.* Accessed December 23, 2017 at *oxfordreference.com.*
2. "George W. Bush Declares Mission Accomplished," in "Speeches & Audio," *History.* Accessed December 9, 2017 at *history.com.*
3. Jefferson Morley, "The Land of the Free and the Home of the Brave," *The Globalist,* July 4, 2013. Accessed at *theglobalist.com.*

Plate 46
Violin Tax?

1. John Yoo, "Terrorists Have No Geneva Rights," *Wall Street Journal,* May 26, 2004. Accessed December 3, 2017 at *aei.org.*
2. Seymour M. Hersh, "Torture at Abu Ghraib. American soldiers brutalized Iraqis. How far up does the responsibility go?," *The New Yorker,* May 10, 2004. Accessed at *newyorker.com.*

Plate 47
Concealed Kerry

1. Jonah Goldberg, "Kerry, Kerry Quite Contrary," *National Review,* November 1, 2006. Accessed at *nationalreview.com.*
2. John Forbes Kerry, *Geneanet.* Accessed December 7, 2017 at *gw.geneanet.org.*
3. "John Kerry on His Catholic Faith in 2004 Third Presidential Debate," *Berkley Center for Religion, Peace & World Affairs, Georgetown University,* October 13, 2004. Accessed at *berkleycenter.georgetown.edu.*
4. Michael Kranish, "A long obscured branch on John Kerry's family tree," *Boston Globe,* October 13, 2013. Accessed at *bostonglobe.com.*
5. Michael Kranish, "Yale grades portray Kerry as a lackluster student," *boston.com News,* June 7, 2005. Accessed at *archive.boston.com.*
6. David Greenberg, "Bred in Their Skull and Bones," *The Washington Post,* February 29, 2004. Accessed at *The Washington Post (WP Company LLC).*
7. Ibid.
8. Thornton McEnery, "The best of the rest. . ." in "The 15 Most Powerful Members of 'Skull And Bones,' " *BUSINESS INSIDER,* February 20, 2011. Accessed at *businessinsider.com.*
9. Nicolas D. Kristof, "A War Hero or a Phony?," *The New York Times,* September 18, 2004. Accessed at *nytimes.com.*
10. "swiftboating," *Urban Dictionary.* Accessed December 8, 2017 at *urbandictionary.com.*
11. Brian Ross and Chris Vlasto, "Did Kerry Discard Vietnam Medals?," *ABC News.* Accessed December 8, 2017 at *abcnews.go.com.*
12. "Kerry discusses $87 billion comment," *CNN,* September 30, 2004. Accessed at *cnn.com.*

Plate 48
Blood Libel

1. "What does 'blood libel' mean?" *BBC News,* January 1, 2011. Accessed at *bbc.com.*
2. "Best States for Gun Owners 2014," *Guns & Ammo,* May 22, 2014. Accessed at *gunsandammo.com.*
3. *The Holy Bible, New International Version,* (Grand Rapids, Michigan: Zondervan, 2011).
4. "Jews Blood Rumor (Did a Saudi Arabian newspaper run an article claiming that Jews use the blood of Christians and Muslims in foods created to celebrate the Jewish holiday of Purim?)," *Snopes.* Accessed December 3, 2017 at *snopes.com.*

WHITE LIES MATTER

Plate 49
Patriotic Assets

1. David Sherfinski, "Donald Trump: 'Ungrateful traitor Chelsea Manning should never have been released.' " *The Washington Times,* January 26, 2017. Accessed at *washingtontimes.com.*
2. Edward Jay Epstein, "Why President Obama Can't Pardon Edward Snowdon," *Newsweek,* January 5, 2017. Accessed at *newsweek.com.*
3. "Matthew 16:19," *The Holy Bible, New International Version,* (Grand Rapids, Michigan: Zondervan, 2011).

Plate 50
Beneath the Pale

1. David Brooks, "The Oil Plume," *The New York Times,* May 31, 2010. Accessed at *nytimes.com.*
2. *"Our history,"* BPGlobal. Accessed November 27, 2017 at *bp.com.*
3. Mike Soraghan, "Companies Involved in Gulf Oil Spill Play 'Name That Disaster' With Eye on Posterity," *The New York Times,* September 9, 2010. Accessed at *nytimes.com.*
4. Steven Mufson, "Halliburton to Pay $1.1 Billion to Settle Gulf Oil Spill Lawsuits," *The Washington Post,* September 2, 2014. Accessed at *The Washington Post (WP Company LLC).*
5. Campbell Robertson and Clifford Krauss, *"Gulf Spill Is the Largest of Its Kind Scientists Say,"* The New York Times, August 2, 2010. Accessed at *nytimes.com.*
6. Brian Clark Howard, "BP Oil Spill Trashed More Shoreline Than Scientists Thought," *National Geographic,* April 20, 2016. Accessed at *news.nationalgeographic.com.*
7. Ibid
8. Ibid.
.

Plate 51
The Continuing Crusade

1. Kevin Liptak, "Obama says Syria war 'haunts' him," *CNN,* September 22, 2016. Accessed at *cnn.com.*

Plate 52
The Caged Bird Sings

1. Lonnae O'Neal, "Maya Angelou's new stamp uses a quote that may not be entirely hers," *The Washington Post,* April 6, 2015. Accessed at *The Washington Post (WP Company LLC).*
2. "Maya Angelou stamp features quote that isn't hers," *CBS News,* April 7, 2015. Accessed at *cbsnews.com.*
3. Lisa Respers France, "Oops: Quote on Maya Angelou's stamp isn't hers," *CNN,* April 8, 2015. Accessed at *cnn.com.*
4. J. Hirby, "What Are Some Consequences Of Plagiarism?," *The Law Dictionary.* Accessed November 27, 2017 at *the lawdictionary.org.*
5. "5 Great People Who Plagiarized," *PT Plagiarism Today,* February 10, 2015. Accessed at *plagiarismtoday.com.*

Plate 53
The Junior Varsity

1. Brendon Bordelon, "Clinton Defends Obama's 'JV Team' label for ISIS," *National Review,* November 19, 2015. Accessed at *nationalreview.com.*
2. Steve Contorno, "What Obama said about Islamic State as a 'JV' team," *Politifact,* September 7, 2014. Accessed at *politifact.com.*
3. Hayes Brown, "Obama Walks Back Comments Downplaying Power of Terror Group," *ThinkProgress,* September 4, 2014. Accessed at *thinkprogress.org.*
5. Marlow Stern, "Kobe Bryant's Disturbing Rape Case: The DNA Evidence, the Accuser's Story, and the Half-Confession," *The Daily Beast,* April 11, 2016. Accessed at *thedailybeast.com.*
6. Kurt Helin, "Stunning Revelation: Magic Johnson Had Sex," *NBC Sports,* February 14, 2010. Accessed at *nba.nbcsports.com.*

Plate 54
The Legacy

1. William Kristol, "Obama's Legacy," *The Weekly Standard,* May 1, 2017. Accessed at *weeklystandard.com.*
2. Ibid.
3. Michael Grunwald, "The Nation He Built," *Politico Magazine,* January/February 2016. Accessed at *politico.com.*
4. Ibid.
5. "10 Historians on What Will Be Said About President Obama's Legacy," *Time,* January 20, 2017. Accessed at *time.com.*
6. Ibid.
7. Ibid.

White Lies Matter

Plate 55
TrumpupPence

1. Jia Tolentino, "Mike Pence's Marriage and the Beliefs That Keep Women from Power," *The New Yorker,* March 31, 2017. Accessed at *newyorker.com*.
2. Ursula Faw, "Mike Pence is a Theocrat. His Christian Supremacist Followers Seek To Take Over America. Seriously," January 2, 2017, *Daily Kos*. Accessed at *Kos Media LLC*.
3. Jonathan Mahler and Dirk Johnson, "Mike Pence's Journey: Catholic Democrat to Evangelical Republican," The New York Times, July 20, 2016. Accessed December 11 2017 at nytimes.com.
4. Brian Eason, "Trump's VP: 10 things to know about Mike Pence," Indy Star, Updated January 18, 2017. Accessed at indystar.com.
5. Faw, "Mike Pence,"
6. Ibid.
7. Ibid.
8. James Glanz, and Alissa J. Rubin, "From Errand to Fatal Shot to Hail of ire to 17 Deaths," *The New York Times,* October 3, 2007. Accessed at *nytimes.com*.
9. Jeremy W. Peters, Maggie Haberman and Glenn Thrush, "Erik Prince, Blackwater Founder, Weighs Primary Challenge to Wyoming Republican," *The New York Times,* October 8, 2017. Accessed at *nytimes.com*
10. Glanz, "From Errand."
11. Faw, "Mike Pence."

Plate 56
Ill Eagle

1. Tom Kertscher, "Is Donald Trump the only major-party nominee in 40 years not to release his tax returns?," *Politifact,* September 28, 2016. Accessed at *politifact.com*.
2. Michael Kranish, "A fierce will to win pushed Donald Trump to the top," *The Washington Post,* January 19, 2017. Accessed at *washingtonpost.com*.
3. Jonathon Martin, and Alan Rappeport, "Donald Trump Says John McCain Is No War Hero, Setting Off Another Storm," *The New York Times, July 18, 2015.* Accessed at *nytimes.com*.

Plate 57
The Beat Goes On

1. Paul Ballanger, "12 Best Chain coffee Shops in America," October 7, 2014, *Coffee Makers USA*. Accessed at *coffee-makersusa.com*.
2. " 'Retail Racism' : 2 black men arrested at Starbucks get an apology from police," April 20, 2018 (updated), *DAWN*. Accessed at *dawn.com*.
3. Tom Head, "Racial Profiling in the United States," March 17, 2017 (updated), *ThoughtCo*. Accessed at *thoughtco.com*.
4. Robert Staples, "White Power, Black Crime, and Racial Politics," November 10, 2015, *The Black Scholar,* vol. 41, no. 4, 31. Accessed at *tandfonline.com*.
5. Scott Calvert, "Philadelphia Police Chief Apologizes for Starbucks Incident," *The Wall Street Journal,* April 19, 2018 (updated). Accessed at *wsj.com*.
6. Ibid.

Plate 58
Your Nation

1. "Yellow Journalism," *Thesaurus.com*. Accessed at *thesaurus.com*.
2. "U.S. Diplomacy and Yellow Journalism, 1895-1898," in "Milestones:1866-1898," *Office of the Historian*. Accessed April 21, 2018 at *history.state.gov*.
3. Ibid.
4. "Yellow Journalism: William Randolph Hearst,", *PBS*. Accessed on April 21, 2018 at *pbs.org*.
5. "Yellow Journalism: The 'Fake News' of the 19th Century," *The Public Domain Review*. Accessed April 21, 2018 at *publicdomainreview.org*.
6. *The American Printer,* July 5,1917, 47. Accessed April 21, 2018 at *books.google.com*.
7. Seymour Topping, "Biography of Joseph Pulitzer," *The Pulitzer Prizes*. Accessed April 21, 2018 at *pulitzer.org*.

Plate 59
We're Number One?

1. Gary Price, MD, and Tim Norbeck, "U.S. Health Outcomes Compared to Other Countries Are Misleading," *Forbes,* April 9, 2018. Accessed at *forbes.com.*
2. Ibid.
3. Ibid.
4. Ibid.
5. Ibid.
6. Ibid.
7. Ibid
8. Josh Holder, Paul Torpey and Fielding Cage, "How does the US healthcare system compare with other countries?," *The Guardian,* July 25, 2017. Accessed at *theguardian. com.*
9. "World Health Organization's Ranking of the World's Health Systems," The Patient Factor, May 24, 2018. Accessed at *thepatientfactor.com.*
10. Bradley Sawyer and Cynthia Cox, "How does health spending in the U.S. compare to other countries?," *Peterson-Kaiser Health System Tracker.* Accessed on May 24, 2018 at *healthsystemtracker.org.*
11. "Japan Has The Highest Life Expectancy Of Any Major Country. Why?," *NBC News,* June 13, 2014. Accessed at *nbcnews.com.*

Plate 60
Who Knew?

1. U.S. Constitution, Section 4 Article III.
2. "2018 World Press Freedom Index," *Reporters without Borders.* Accessed May 25, 2018 at *rsf.org.*
3. Michael J. Abramowitz, "Hobbling a Champion of Global Press Freedom," *Freedom House.* Accessed May 25, 2018 at *freedomhouse.org.*
4. Ibid.
5. Ibid.
6. Ibid.

CPSIA information can be obtained
at www.ICGtesting.com
Printed in the USA
BVHW021817070321
601957BV00020B/907